Dolly Bureau

volume 2

Doll Patterns and Fashion

Megann R. Zabel

Table of Contents:

Pattern on pages 87-89

Pattern
on pages
87-89

Photograph © MegannArt
PukiPuki Sugar made by FairyLand. http://dollfairyland.com/

Photograph © MegannArt
Fashion Royalty® made by Integrity Toys, Inc. www.integritytoys.com

Pattern
on pages
80-83

Pattern
on pages
66-68

FR2 body
pattern
on pages
72-74

FR body
pattern
on pages
72-74

Pattern
on pages
69-71

Pattern on pages 78-79

Pattern
on pages
64-65

FR body
pattern
on pages
60-61

FR2 body
pattern
on pages
60-61

Pattern
on pages
90-91

Pattern on pages 84-86

Pattern
& tutorial
on pages
54-59

Pattern
on pages
62-63

Photograph © Megan
Fairy of Fairytales Cheshire Goon made by Peak's Woods. www.peakswoods

Pattern
on pages
75-77

Doll

Comparison

Photos

Monthly
Fairy in
Super Tiny
BJD
Dress

26

Picco Neemo in Super Tiny BJD Outfit

Pinkie Cooper in Super Slim 10.5 Inch Doll Skirt & Tiny BJD Dress

29

La Dee
Da in
Super Slim
10.5 Inch
Doll
Design

Silkstone
Barbie in
FR/FR2
Design

31

Tonner
Deja Vu
in 1:6
Scale BJD
Designs

Photograph © MegannAr
Deja Vu™ doll used by permission of Tonner Doll Company, Inc. www.tonnerdoll.com

Picco Neemo in Super Tiny BJD Dress

33

Kelly &
Friends
in Super
Tiny BJD
Designs

34

Limhwa
Sara in
momoko
Design

Honee-B
in Super
Tiny BJD
Dress

Tonner
Revlon
in 1:6
Scale BJD
Design

Izzy (Amelia Thimble) in Super Tiny BJD Design

Mod Era
Barbie in
FR/FR2
Outfit

Photograph © Meç
Barbie® Mat

Doll Comparison Sizes

The patterns in this book have been sized specifically for certain dolls (listed below in bold); however, depending on the pattern, it **may** fit other dolls. Please see the list below for other dolls that **may** fit these patterns.

12 inch fashion dolls (Fashion Royalty doll): Some other Integrity 12 inch dolls, Model Muse, Mod Era Barbie, Silkstone Barbie, some other Barbie sizes.

Super slim 10.5 inch dolls (Monster High doll): La Dee Da, Disney V.I.P., Ever After High, Pinkie Cooper, Ai Ball-Jointed Doll, and Licca.

momoko: Blythe, Susie, Limhwa 27 cm tall ball-jointed dolls (such as Mari & Sara), J-doll, Pullip, Skipper, Azone Pure Neemo, Jenny, Liv.

1:6 scale ball-jointed dolls: Variety of "YoSD" sized ball-jointed dolls (approximately 26 cm in height), Soom Rosette (small bust) Tonner Revlon, and Tonner Deja Vu.

Super tiny ball-jointed dolls: Variety of 10-12 cm sized ball-jointed dolls (such as Ruby Red Galleria's Honee-B, Peak's Woods Monthly Fairies, Fairyland PukiPuki, and Lati White), Dollcena, Pinkie Cooper, Picco Neemo, Kelly (Barbie's little sister), Little Pullip, Petite Blythe, and Amelia Thimble.

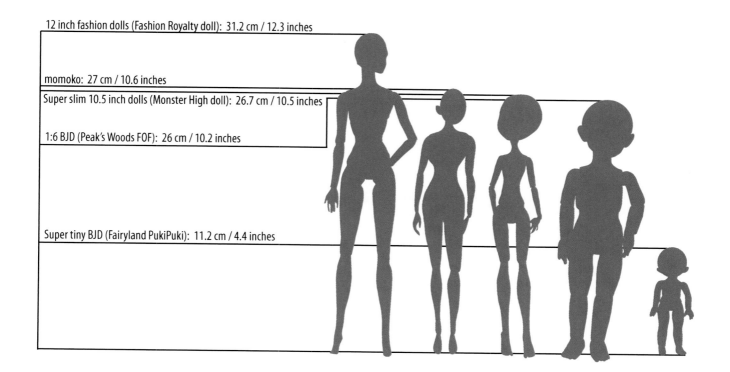

12 inch fashion dolls (Fashion Royalty doll): 31.2 cm / 12.3 inches

momoko: 27 cm / 10.6 inches

Super slim 10.5 inch dolls (Monster High doll): 26.7 cm / 10.5 inches

1:6 BJD (Peak's Woods FOF): 26 cm / 10.2 inches

Super tiny BJD (Fairyland PukiPuki): 11.2 cm / 4.4 inches

Understanding This Book:

Experience Level:
This pattern book is beginner to intermediate. Some basic sewing experience is recommended. Jewelry-making experience is helpful as well.

Reading Patterns:
Below are some basic guidelines in understanding the formatting and directions for patterns in this book.

1. All pattern pieces throughout the book will have a CAPITALIZED label, including in the directions.
2. Please see the box below for a legend of sewing symbols on patterns.
3. All patterns are meant for hook-and-loop, hook-and-eye, or bead-and-loop fasteners. See *Closures* section on pages 47-50.

FOLD ▷▷	Fold both pattern and fabric in half for full-sized pattern piece
○—	Ending point for seam for placement of closure
⊕	Bead-and-loop or hook-and-eye closure
∇∇∇∇∇	Zigzag stitch
▪▪▪ ▪▪▪ ▪▪▪	Elastic
∿∿	Gather fabric
··········	Top stitch or similar stitch
↕	Direction of fabric design
───	Seam allowance
— — —	Fold line

Tracing and Cutting Patterns:
To trace patterns without cutting up this book, trace all features of pattern using tissue paper. Cut out pattern pieces. Pin the tissue paper to desired fabric and cut out each piece before beginning the sewing directions.

Sewing Pattern Basics:

For most of the patterns in this book, the below items will be required. In the directions for each pattern, there will be a "sewing pattern basics" notation. Refer to the list below for pattern requirements.

1. **Tissue paper** and **pen** for tracing patterns. See *Tracing and Cutting Patterns* on page 45.
2. **Fabric** to fit pattern pieces. Every pattern in this book requires less than 1 yard of fabric and/or trim, unless otherwise specified in pattern directions.
3. **Sewing machine** with appropriate **machine needles**.
4. **Sewing needles, thread, and sewing pins**. A variety of hand-sewing needle sizes may be helpful. For instance, tiny buttons and seed beads in some patterns may require special needles, like a beading needle.
5. **Scissors**.
6. **Iron**. Pressing edges makes a garment look finished and clean. However, some fabrics may not be iron-friendly.

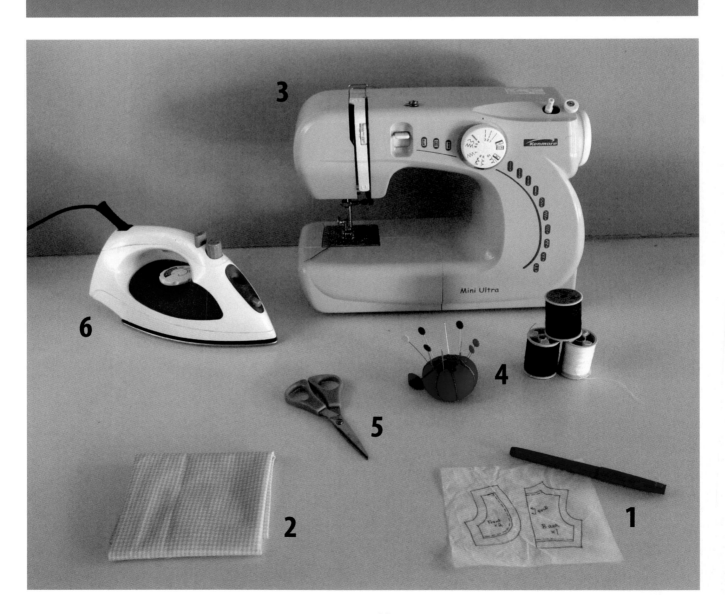

Optional Sewing Items:

Some of the items below are helpful and recommended, although not necessarily required.

1. **Hemostats**. Turning inside out those tiny sleeves can be difficult. Using hemostats makes it much easier.
2. **Seam ripper**. Pull out threads easily with this tool.
3. **Measuring tape**. This can be helpful if resizing or double checking lengths of pattern pieces. Some patterns require cutting a certain length of ribbon or lace, which may need to be measured. See the back of this book for a basic ruler.
4. **Disappearing ink marking pen** or **other fabric-marking tool**, such as **chalk**. Marking seams, darts, and other special notations on pattern with a fabric-marking tool will ensure accurate results. Be sure to test the marking pen on fabric before tracing out an entire pattern.
5. **Rotary cutter.** This tool will help cut larger pieces of fabric quickly. The cutting mat used with a rotary cutting tool is not pictured.
6. **Anti-fray adhesive** (not pictured). Some of those edges in fabric will try to fray even though they are on the inside of the garment. Using an anti-fray adhesive like Dritz Fray Check can help reduce fraying.

Note: Other items may be required for patterns. Please see individual pattern "supplies" lists for further information.

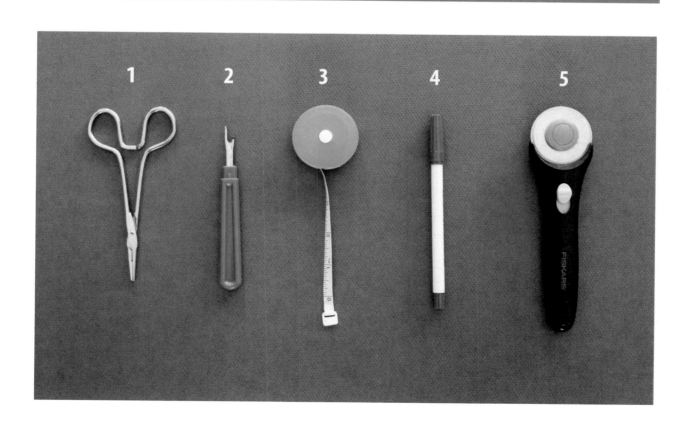

Sewing Terminology Defined:

Basting stitch: Loosely applying a temporary sewing stitch to hold layers of fabric in place. This method can be helpful, especially if trying to *ease* fabric.

Ease: Bring fabrics together to fit an area without causing any puckers. Sewing pins or a *basting stitch* are helpful for this task.

Gather: Shortening the length of fabric so that the gathered (longer) piece of fabric can be attached to a shorter piece. The effect is often meant to create fullness in a garment.

Loop turner: Slender tool, often metal, used to pull fabric through small tunnel-like fabrics, such as a strap, button loop, or frog closure.

Ruffle: Gathered or goffered lace or other cloth textile used ornamentally on a garment.

Running stitch: Basic line of stitches achieved by passing a needle in and out of fabric without overlapping the stitch.

Top stitch: Stitching close to the edge or seam on the top (also known as "right side") of the garment.

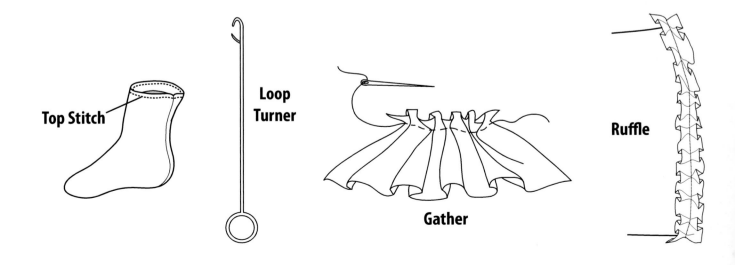

Top Stitch

Loop Turner

Gather

Ruffle

Closures:

All patterns in this book are meant for bead-and-loop, hook-and-eye, or hook-and-loop fasteners. Please see the diagram below for closure materials used on the patterns in this book.

1. **Bead-and-loop closure**. Very affordable method of using crocheting twine tied into a loop and a bead.
2. **Hook-and-eye closure.** This is an alternative to the bead-and-loop closure, but uses the same directions for seams and top stitching.
3. **Hook-and-loop closure.** Commonly known as Velcro. This is more helpful when longer closures are needed.
4. **Snaps.** The patterns in this book **do not** have allowances for fabric to overlap for fasteners like snaps. If snaps are desired, see page 50 for a guide on how to alter patterns to accommodate snap closures.

See the following pages for directions on using closures.

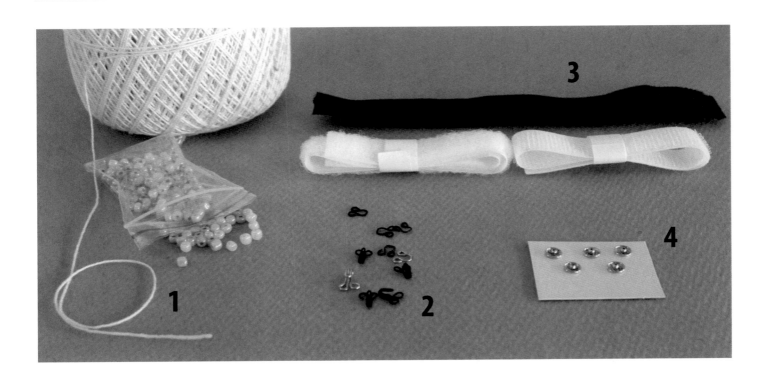

Closure Directions:

Refer to this page and the following for appropriate closure directions on selected doll garments.

Bead-and-loop (Figure A): Fold over remaining raw edges and top stitch, starting from the top part of one side of the opening, down to the seam, over the seam, and up to the end of the folded edges. Tie a loop from crochet thread that will fit snugly over the bead. Hand sew a bead-and-loop closure where indicated.

Hook-and-eye closures (Figure A): Use same directions as above, replacing the type of closure with a hook-and-eye.

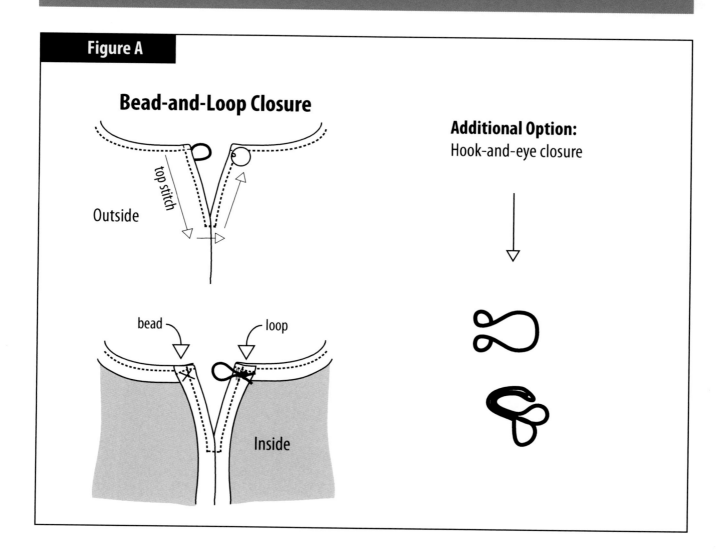

Figure A

Bead-and-Loop Closure

top stitch

Outside

bead

loop

Inside

Additional Option:
Hook-and-eye closure

Hook-and-Loop Closure Tape
(seam at opening)

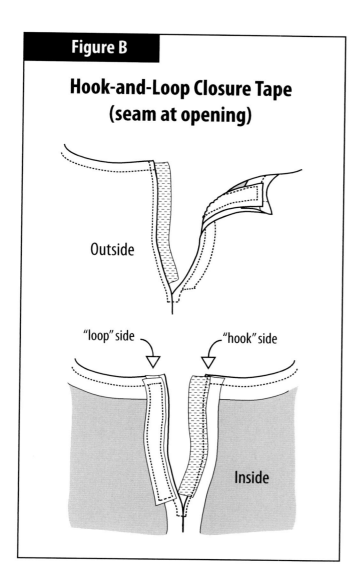

Figure C

Hook-and-Loop Closure Tape
(no seam at opening)

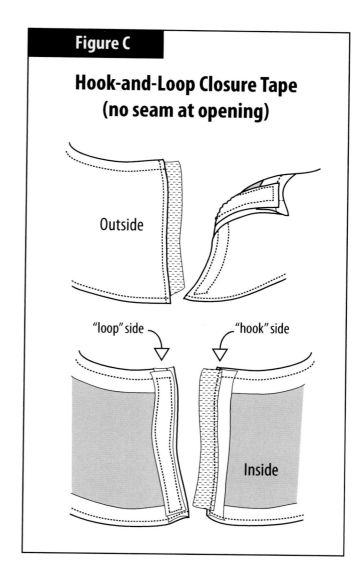

Hook-and-loop closures:

Seam at opening (Figure B): Fold over remaining raw edges. Measure out enough closure tape for the opening. Place the "hook" side of the hook-and-loop tape just on the inside enough to top stitch. Make sure the hooked part of the closure is facing out. Top stitch over the closure, starting from the top part of one side of the opening, down to the seam, over the seam, and up to the end of the folded edges. Place the whole looped side of the hook-and-loop tape on the inside of the garment and top stitch in a rectangle, making sure to go over the previously created top stitch.

No seam at opening (Figure C): Fold over remaining raw edges. Measure out enough closure tape for the opening. Place the "hook" side of the hook-and-loop tape just on the inside enough to top stitch. Make sure the hooked part of the closure is facing out. Top stitch hooked tape to garment. Place the whole looped side of the hook-and-loop tape on the inside of the garment and top stitch in a rectangle.

Altering Pattern to Use Snaps:

The patterns in this book do not have allowances for fabric to overlap for snaps. If snaps are desired, please see this tutorial on how to alter patterns to accommodate snap closures.

Adjust Pattern (Figure A): Find closure opening on pattern. Take out **one** side of the pattern, about double the width of the original seam. Be aware that multiple pattern pieces may be involved in the closure seam and will need to be taken out as well, such as a belt in a skirt.

Finish Closure (Figure B): See step-by-step directions below.

1. Fold over seam that has been extended and top stitch to ——o point on pattern.
2. Fold over opposite seam and top stitch to ——o point on pattern.
3. With right sides together, sew seam from bottom of garment to ——o point on pattern. When sewing this seam, make sure raw edges of bottom of garment are flush with each other, not the folded edges on the top of the garment.
4. Top stitch right at seam opening for extra support of seam and to prevent tearing.
5. Hand sew snaps where indicated.

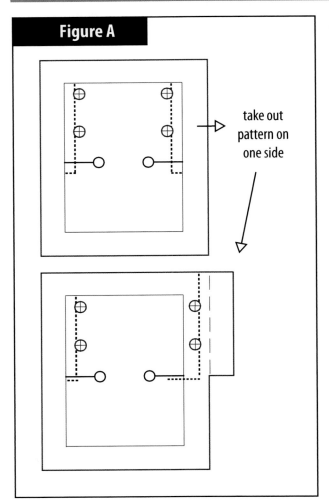

Figure A

take out pattern on one side

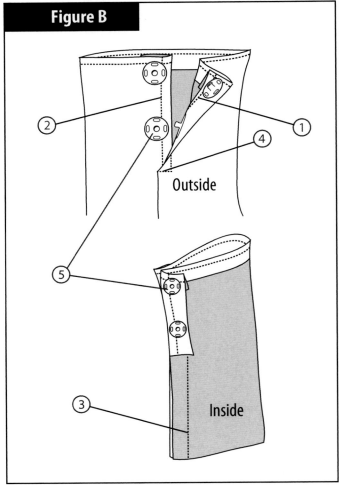

Figure B

Outside

Inside

Helpful Tips and Hints:

Tiny Seams:
Are those seam lines too small? Cut seams larger than pattern and after the seam has been sewn, trim down the seam to the original pattern size.

Stretch Fabric Techniques (Figure A):
If a fabric needs to maintain the stretch to fit onto a doll, such as the waist of leggings, consider using a zigzag stitch rather than a straight stitch. Also, consider using a ball-point or stretch needle in a sewing machine so stitches are not skipped, which is often a problem when using stretch fabrics.

Tissue to the Rescue:
Does the sewing machine "eat" the fabric and/or stretch it out too much? Prevent these issues by using a layer of tissue paper between the machine and the bottom of the fabric. This will help with problems related to fabric being fed through a sewing machine.

Choosing Fabrics:
To obtain realistic-looking designs, aim for small prints and lightweight fabrics. Often, the smaller the doll, the need for a lightweight fabric increases.

Pins versus Basting (Figure B):
Not sure what technique is best to use? Pins are a quick solution and save time, but basting often provides cleaner lines and better results. Also, pins can damage a sewing machine if not taken out before feeding fabric.

Patterns for Other Dolls :
Planning on trying a pattern out on another type of doll other than what is listed in this book? Consider using fabrics that have some stretch or "give," such a jersey. This will ensure a better fit if stretch is needed for a different doll body type.

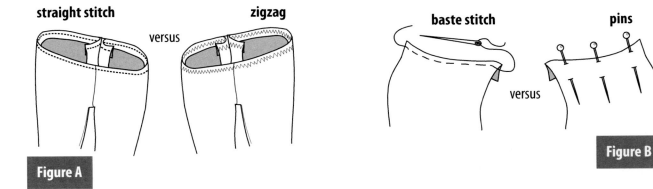

straight stitch   versus   zigzag

Figure A

baste stitch   versus   pins

Figure B

Patterns

Pajama Top Tutorial

Photos on pages 18-19.

Supplies:
Sewing pattern basics (See pages 44-45)
Bead-and-loop closures
Tiny buttons or seed beads
Ribbon (3 mm wide or less)
Lace trim

Pattern Pieces (on page 59):
TOP FRONT x1, TOP BACK x2, SLEEVE x2, BOTTOM x1, and RUFFLE x1

Steps:
Before following the steps outlined in the diagram, cut enough of each pattern piece for this pajama top. A satin-like fabric was used for the pajama top. Lightweight fabrics are recommended for this project.

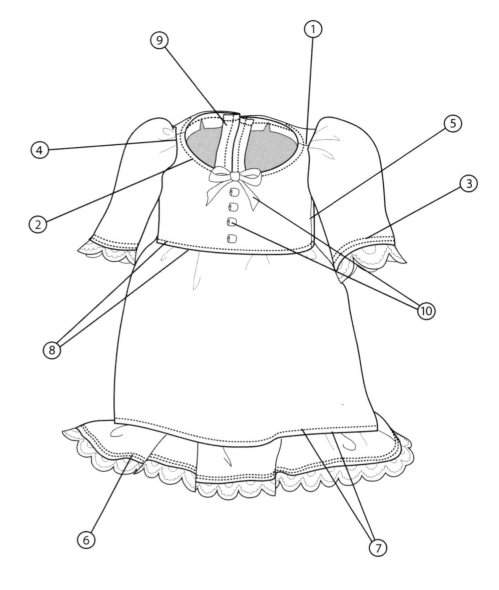

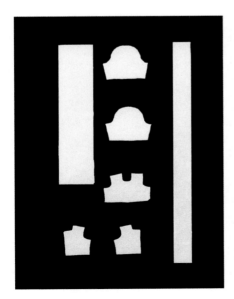

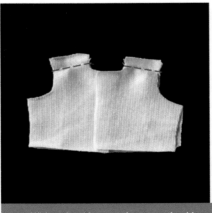

1. With right sides together, sew shoulder seams of TOP FRONT to TOP BACK pieces.

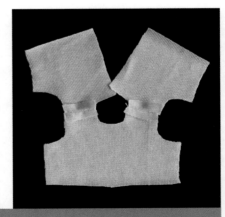

Press seams open.

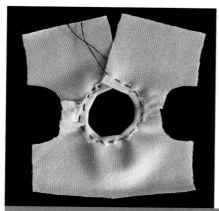

2. Clip curved edges of neck opening. Fold over neck opening of TOP FRONT and TOP BACK pieces and pin in place or baste stitch.

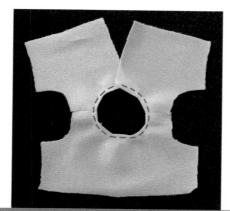

Top stitch over folded edge.

3. Fold over SLEEVE bottom and press with iron. Cut enough lace trim for the length of the SLEEVE opening.

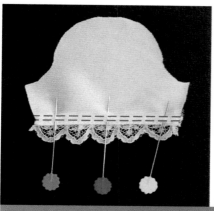

Pin lace trim in place on back of garment and top stitch two rows of stitches. Repeat with other SLEEVE piece.

4. Gather upper SLEEVE where indicated, matching the length of the gather to the armhole length. Ease upper SLEEVE into each armhole using sewing pins or basting stitch.

With right sides together, sew seam and repeat for other SLEEVE.

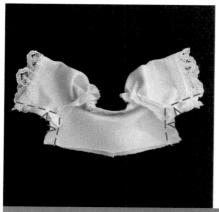

5. With right sides together, sew seam from one armhole opening, to the armpit, then down to join the TOP FRONT and TOP BACK pieces. Clip curves around armpit area. Repeat for other side.

Turn sleeves inside out.

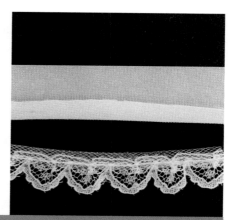

6. Fold over RUFFLE bottom and press with iron. Cut enough lace trim for the long length of the RUFFLE.

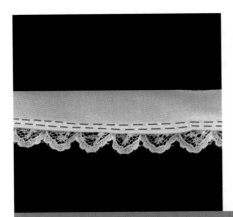

Pin lace trim in place on back of garment and top stitch two rows of stitches.

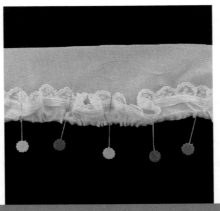

7. On RUFFLE piece, gather where indicated until gather is the length of the bottom of the BOTTOM piece. With right sides together, pin gathered fabric every 1/2 inch to inch. Sew seam.

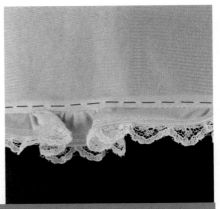

Fold seam of RUFFLE and BOTTOM pieces up and top stitch over BOTTOM piece.

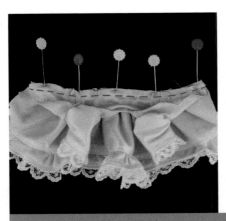

8. On BOTTOM piece, gather top until gather is the length of the bottom of the TOP FRONT and TOP BACK pieces. With right sides together, pin gathered fabric every 1/2 inch to inch. Sew seam.

Fold seam of BOTTOM, TOP FRONT and TOP BACK pieces up and top stitch.

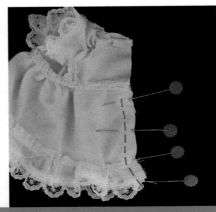

9. With right sides together, sew seam from bottom of back of SKIRT up to ——O point on pattern. Turn inside out.

Fold over remaining raw edges and top stitch, starting from the top part of one side of the opening, down to the seam, over the seam, and up to the end of the folded edges.

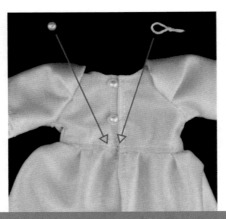

Where indicated, hand sew a bead-and-loop closure. See pages 47-50 for a helpful *Closures* guide.

10. Make a bow out of 3 mm wide ribbon. Using a needle and thread, sew bow and a row of seed beads or tiny buttons to the center front of the TOP FRONT piece.

Pajama Bloomers Tutorial

Photos on pages 18-19.

Supplies:
Sewing pattern basics (See pages 44-45)
Elastic, 1/4 inch wide or less
Lace trim

Pattern Pieces (on page 59):
BLOOMERS x2

Steps:
Before following the steps outlined in the diagram, cut enough of each pattern piece for these bloomers. A satin-like fabric was used for the bloomers. Lightweight fabrics are recommended for this project.

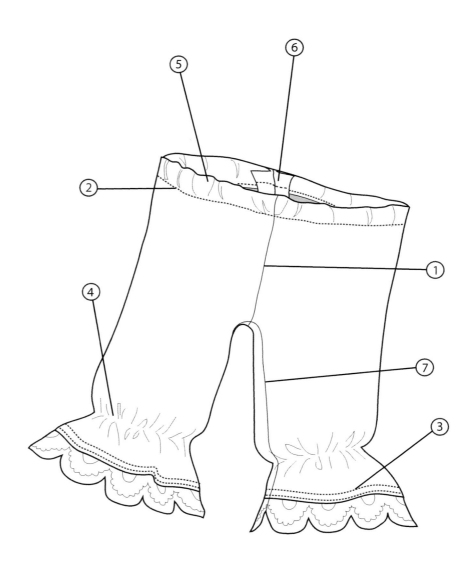

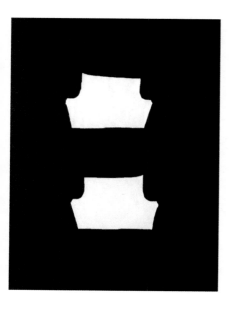

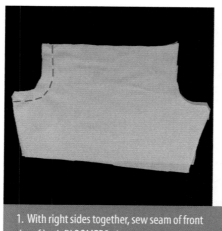

1. With right sides together, sew seam of front rise of both BLOOMERS pieces.

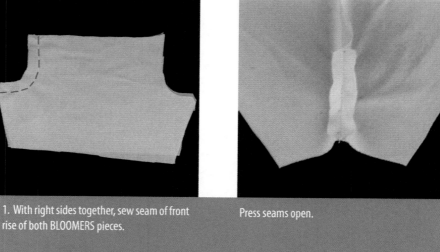

Press seams open.

Pajama Bloomers Tutorial

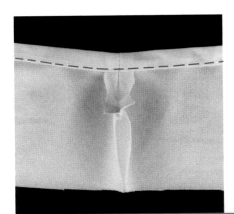

2. Fold top of bloomers over twice and press with iron. Make sure enough room is available in fold to accommodate feeding elastic through. Top stitch close to the bottom edge of fold.

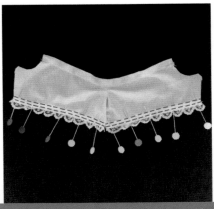

3. Fold over BLOOMERS bottom and press with iron. Cut enough lace for the length of each BLOOMERS bottom. Pin lace in place on back of garment and top stitch two rows of stitches.

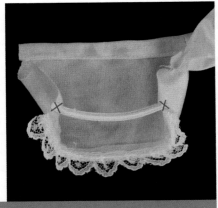

4. Cut two pieces of thin elastic approximately 2-1/4 inches in length. Where indicated to include elastic in bloomers pant leg, baste stitch both ends of elastic in the seam. Repeat for other pant leg.

While stretching the elastic, carefully do a zigzag stitch to hold the elastic in place.

5. Cut approximately 3-1/2 inches of elastic. Double check this length on doll waist. The elastic should stretch quite a bit over the waist. Feed elastic through waist opening with loop turner.

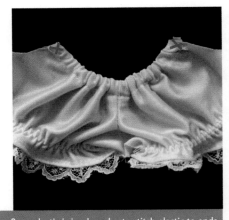

Once elastic is in place, baste stitch elastic to ends of garment to hold in place.

6. With right sides together, sew seam of back rise of both BLOOMERS pieces.

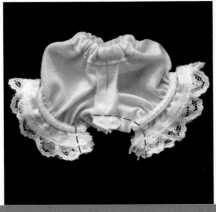

7. With right sides together, sew seam from bottom of one pant leg up to the rise and then down the other pant leg.

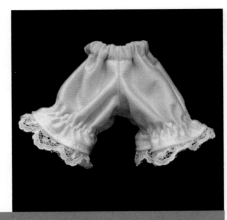

Turn inside out.

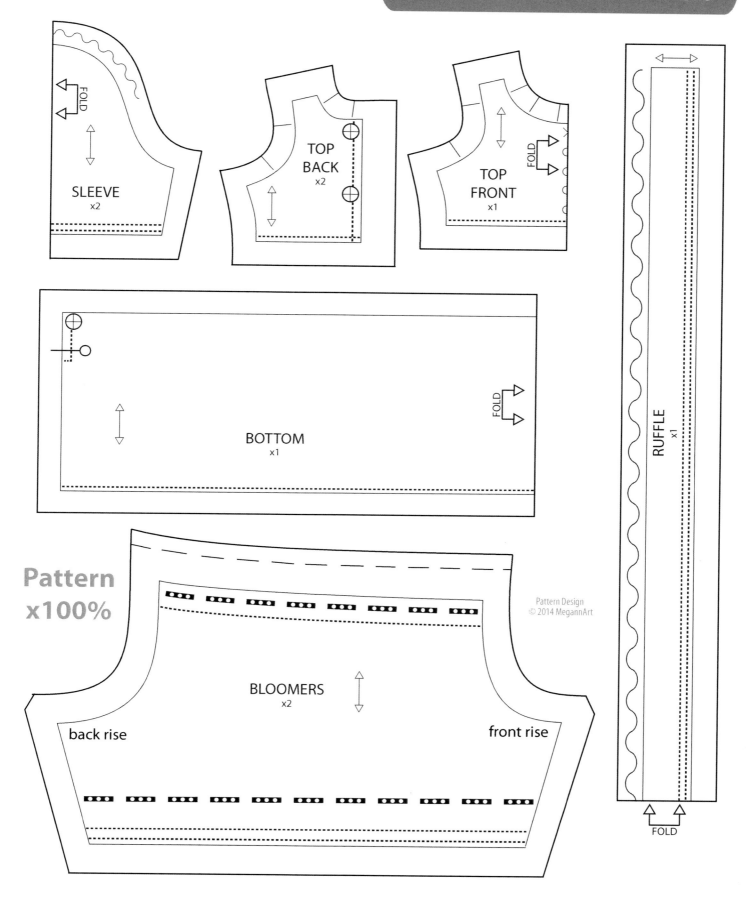

SLEEVE
x2

TOP
BACK
x2

TOP
FRONT
x1

FOLD

FOLD

FOLD

RUFFLE
x1

BOTTOM
x1

FOLD

**Pattern
x100%**

Pattern Design
© 2014 MegannArt

BLOOMERS
x2

back rise

front rise

FOLD

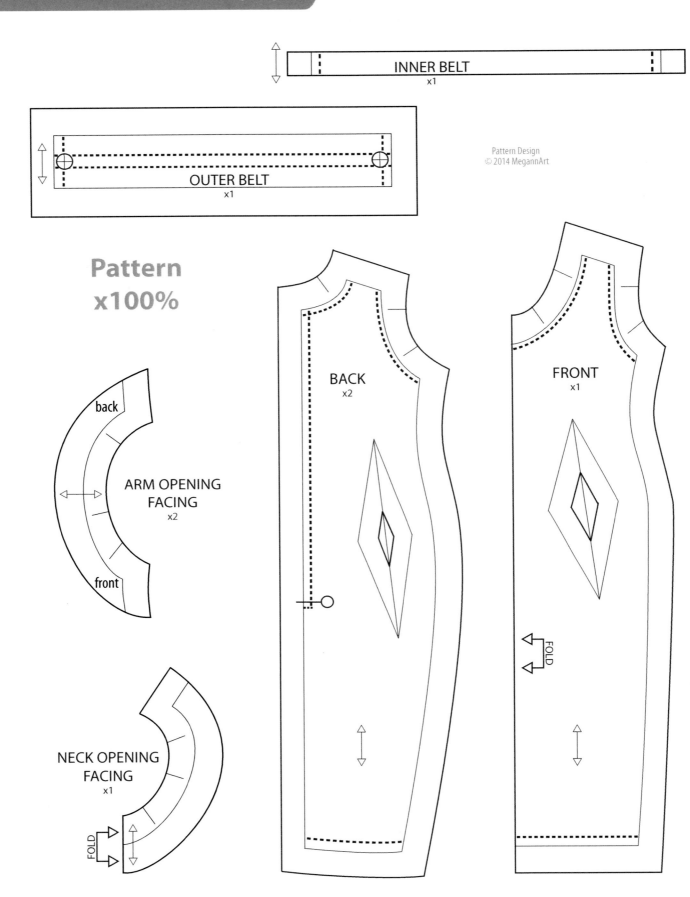

INNER BELT
x1

OUTER BELT
x1

Pattern Design
© 2014 MegannArt

Pattern x100%

BACK
x2

FRONT
x1

FOLD

back

ARM OPENING
FACING
x2

front

NECK OPENING
FACING
x1

FOLD

DRESS:

Photos on pages 14-15.

Pattern Pieces:
FRONT x1, BACK x2, ARM OPENING FACING x2, and NECK OPENING FACING x1

Supplies:
Sewing pattern basics (See pages 44-45)
Hook-and-loop closure

Steps:
Before following the steps outlined in the diagram, cut enough of the pattern piece for this dress. Tulle is recommended for the facing.

NOTE: Facing pattern pieces are optional and pattern can be made without these pieces.

1. Make darts on either side of FRONT piece by folding right side together and sewing along outer seams of dart. Repeat on other side of FRONT piece. Press darts down center. Repeat with darts on BACK pieces.
2. Sew shoulder seams of FRONT to BACK pieces with the right sides together. Press seams open.
3. With right sides together, sew seam of NECK OPENING FACING to the neck opening of the FRONT and BACK pieces. Clip curved edges. Fold all of the facing into wrong side of garment and top stitch neck opening.
4. With right sides together, sew seam of ARM OPENING FACING to the armhole of the FRONT and BACK pieces. Clip curved edges. Fold all of the facing into wrong side of garment and top stitch armhole. Repeat for other side.
5. With right sides together, sew front and back side seams together from the arm opening to the bottom of the garment. Press seams open.
6. Fold over bottom of garment and top stitch.
7. With right sides together, sew seam from bottom of back of dress up to ——O point on pattern. Turn inside out. See pages 47-50 for a bead-and-loop *Closures* guide.

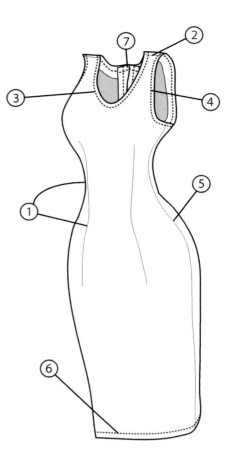

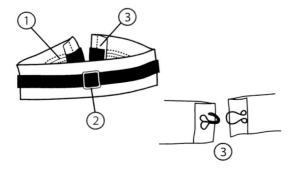

BELT:

Photos on pages 14-15.

Pattern Pieces:
OUTER BELT x1, INNER BELT x1

Supplies:
Sewing pattern basics (See pages 44-45)
Bra slide
Hook-and-loop closure

Steps:
Before following the steps outlined in the diagram, cut enough of the pattern piece for this belt. Thin vinyl was used for the inner belt.

1. Fold long edges of OUTER BELT in and press. Top stitch over each folded edge.
2. Insert bra slide into INNER BELT.
3. Place INNER BELT in middle of OUTER BELT. Fold over back sides of belt over and top stitch. Using a needle and thread, sew hook-and-look closure into back of belt.

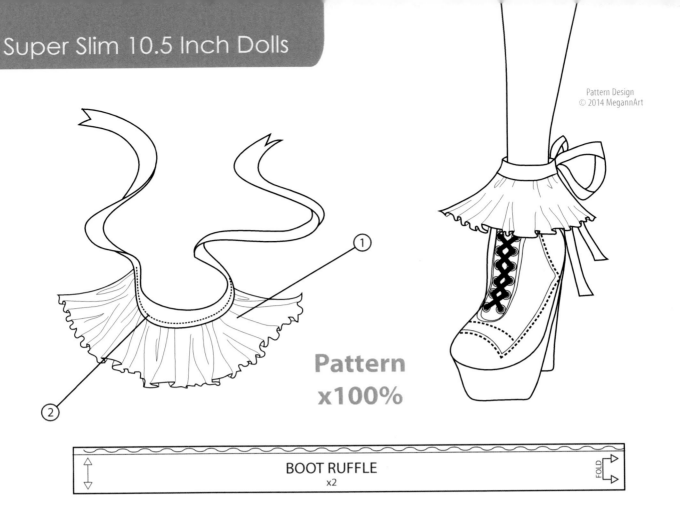

Pattern Design
© 2014 MegannArt

Pattern x100%

① ②

BOOT RUFFLE
x2

FOLD

BOOT RUFFLE:

Photo on page 21.

Pattern Pieces:
BOOT RUFFLE x2

Supplies:
Sewing pattern basics (See pages 44-45)
Approximately 10-12 inches of 3 mm wide ribbon

Steps:
Before following the steps outlined in the diagram, cut enough of each pattern piece for this shoe accessory. Tulle was used for the ruffle.

1. On a BOOT RUFFLE piece, use a basting stitch to gather where indicated until gather is 1-1/2 to 1-3/4 inches. Repeat with other BOOT RUFFLE piece.
2. Cut the 3 mm wide ribbon in half. Each half should measure between 5-6 inches in length. Find the center of the ribbon and pin the center of the right side of the ruffle behind it. Carefully pin the rest of the ruffle to the ribbon, trying not to show the top of the ruffle over the ribbon. Top stitch the ruffle in place behind the ribbon. Two rows of stitches may be necessary. If ruffle peaks over the top of the ribbon, clip off excess. Tie boot ruffle with a bow in the back over a boot.

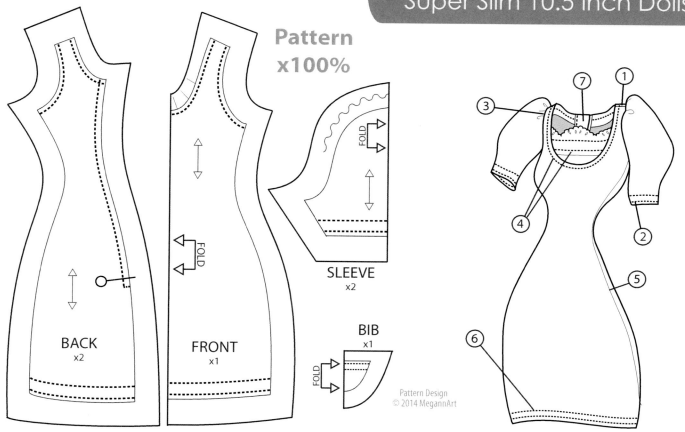

Pattern x100%

BACK
x2

FRONT
x1

SLEEVE
x2

BIB
x1

FOLD

FOLD

Pattern Design
© 2014 MegannArt

DRESS:

Photos on pages 20-21.

Pattern Pieces:
FRONT x1, BACK x2, BIB x1, and SLEEVE x2

Supplies:
Sewing pattern basics (See pages 44-45)
Hook-and-loop tape
Lace trim

Steps:
Before following the steps outlined in the diagram, cut enough of each pattern piece for this dress.

1. Sew shoulder seams of FRONT to BACK pieces with the right sides together. Press seams open.
2. Fold bottom side of each SLEEVE over and top stitch.
3. Gather upper SLEEVE where indicated, trying to match the length of the gather to the FRONT and BACK armhole length. Ease upper SLEEVE into each armhole using sewing pins or a basting stitch. Make sure right sides are together. Sew seam and repeat for other SLEEVE.
4. Fold top of BIB over. Pin lace trim over folded BIB top and top stitch two rows of stitches over the lace trim. In seam, clip curves of neck opening. Fold the neck opening of garment over and place right side of BIB on the wrong side of the top opening. Baste stitch or pin seam and bib in place. Top stitch with two rows of stitches over top opening.
5. With right sides together, sew seam from bottom of SLEEVE to armpit and then to the bottom of the garment. Clip curves, especially under armpit. Press seam from bottom of garment to armpit area. Repeat on other side.
6. Fold over bottom of dress and top stitch with two rows of stitches.
7. With right sides together, sew seam from bottom of BACK pieces up to ○——— point on pattern. Turn inside out. See pages 47-50 for a hook-and-loop *Closures* guide.

Super Tiny BJD (10-12 cm)

ARMHOLE FACING x2

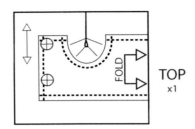

TOP
x1

Pattern x100%

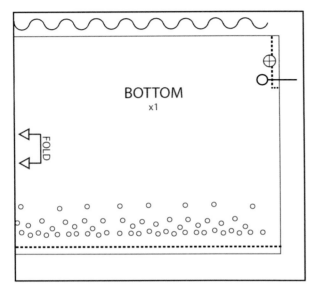

BOTTOM
x1

FOLD

Pattern Design
© 2014 MegannArt

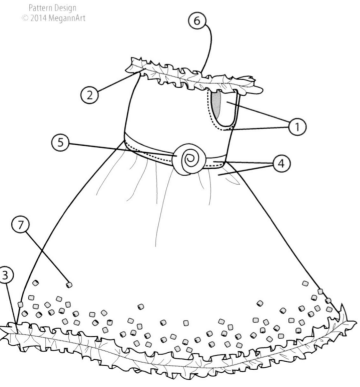

DRESS:

Photo on page 13.

Pattern Pieces:
TOP x1, BOTTOM x1, and ARMHOLE FACING x2.

Supplies:
Sewing pattern basics (See pages 44-45)
Approximately 30 inches of 1/4 inch wide ribbon
Approximately 3 inches of 3 mm wide ribbon
Seed beads
Ribbon rosette
Bead-and-loop closures

Steps:
Before following the steps outlined in the diagram, cut enough of each pattern piece for this dress. Fine mesh tulle fabric is recommended for the ARMHOLE FACING pieces.

SPECIAL NOTE: Depending on the size of the seed beads, a beading needle may be required.

1. With right sides together, sew seam of ARMHOLE FACING to the armhole of the TOP piece. Clip curved edges. Fold all of the facing into wrong side of garment and top stitch armhole. Repeat for other side.
2. Measure out approximately 10 inches of 1/4 wide ribbon. Baste stitch through center of ribbon to make ruffle measuring approximately 3-1/2 inches long. Be sure to test length of ruffle on doll. Fold over top of TOP and find center. Match center of ruffled ribbon and pin in place (Figure A). Work outward from middle and pin in place on TOP piece. On backside of TOP, fold over top and pin ends of ruffled ribbon to end of TOP. Work toward armhole and pin every 1/4 inch. Excess ruffled ribbon should be equally over each armhole. Top stitch ruffle and TOP folded edges along the basting stitch in ribbon. Hand-sewing the top stitch is recommended.
3. Measure out approximately 20 inches of 1/4 wide ribbon. Baste stitch through center of ribbon to make ruffle that measures the same as the long length of the BOTTOM piece. Fold over bottom of BOTTOM and pin ruffled ribbon to bottom of BOTTOM piece. Top stitch along basting stitch in ribbon. Hand-sewing the top stitching is recommended.
4. On the BOTTOM piece, gather where indicated until gather is the length of the bottom of the TOP piece. With right sides together, pin gathered fabric and sew a seam. Cut 3 inches of 3 mm wide ribbon. Fold seam of BOTTOM and TOP pieces up and, with the ribbon pinned in place over the seam, top stitch along the TOP piece of the dress.
5. Place ribbon rose over 3 mm ribbon and stitch in place with a needle and thread.
6. With right sides together, sew seam from bottom of back of dress up to O—— point on pattern. Turn inside out. See pages 47-50 for a bead-and-loop *Closures* guide. Hand-sewing the remaining part of the closure may be helpful since the dress is very small.
7. With a needle and thread, sew seed beads along bottom of dress.

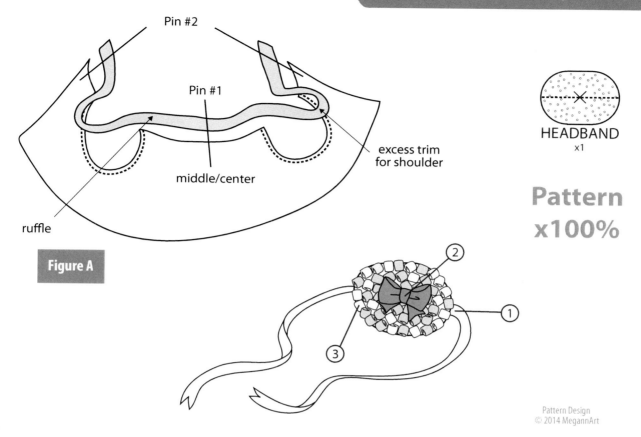

Pin #2

Pin #1

middle/center

excess trim
for shoulder

ruffle

Figure A

HEADBAND
x1

**Pattern
x100%**

① ② ③

HEADBAND:

Photo on page 13.

Pattern Pieces:
HEADBAND x1

Supplies:
Small piece of felt
Needle and thread
Approximately 12 inches of ribbon (3 mm wide)
Seed beads

Steps:
Before following the steps outlined in the diagram, cut out the HEADBAND pattern piece from the felt.

SPECIAL NOTE: Depending on the size of the seed beads, a beading needle may be required.

1. Cut approximately 8 inches of 3 mm wide ribbon for the length of the headband. Cut more ribbon for a head larger than 3-4 inches wide or for a larger bow to tie in the back of the headband. Find the middle of the ribbon and, using a needle and thread, top stitch the HEADBAND piece over the ribbon center.
2. Using the remainder of ribbon, tie a bow. With the needle and thread, sew the bow to the spot marked "X" on the HEADBAND piece.
3. With a needle and thread, completely cover the front surface of the HEADBAND piece by sewing on seed beads.

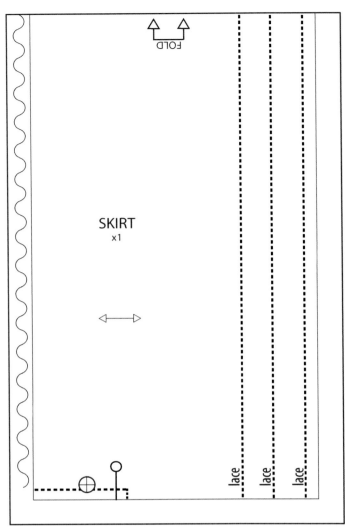

SKIRT
x1

FOLD

lace lace lace

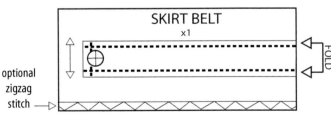

SKIRT BELT
x1

FOLD

optional
zigzag
stitch →

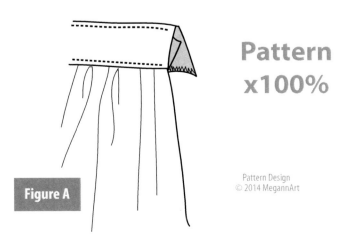

**Pattern
x100%**

Figure A

Pattern Design
© 2014 MegannArt

UNDERSKIRT:

Photo on page 6.

Pattern Pieces:
SKIRT x1 and SKIRT BELT x1

Supplies:
Sewing pattern basics (See pages 44-45)
Bead-and-loop closure
Approximately 39 inches of lace trim

Steps:
Before following the steps outlined in the diagram, cut enough of each pattern piece for this underskirt. SKIRT BELT backside will have a raw edge. Sew an optional zigzag stitch along the backside, where indicated on pattern, if a finished edge is desired. This optional step is not included in the directions below.

The BELT in this skirt will be approximately 4-1/2 inches long when the garment is finished. It is advised to test this length on doll before starting pattern. Add or subtract appropriate amount of length to SKIRT BELT pattern, if necessary.

1. Turn under bottom of SKIRT. Press with iron. Measure out enough lace trim for the length of the bottom of the SKIRT. Pin lace trim piece on front of SKIRT. Top stitch lace trim in place. Measure out two more lace trim pieces of the same length. Note: Lace markers on the pattern may need to be adjusted depending on the size of the lace trim being used. Top stitch each piece just slightly above the lace trim below it.
2. On the SKIRT, gather where indicated until gather is the length of the SKIRT BELT. With right sides together, pin gathered fabric every 1/2 inch to inch to the SKIRT BELT. Sew seam.
3. Fold SKIRT BELT over seam and top stitch along top and bottom of front side of belt (see Figure A).
4. With right sides together, sew seam from bottom of back of SKIRT up to —o point on pattern. Turn inside out. See pages 47-50 for a bead-and-loop *Closures* guide.

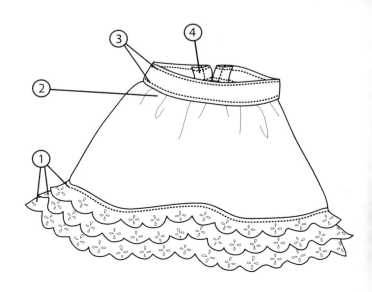

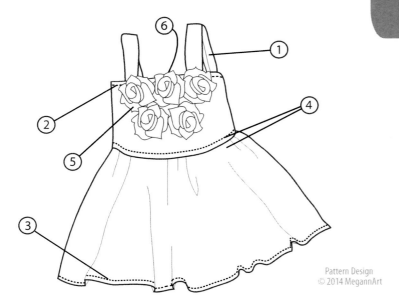

Pattern Design
© 2014 MegannArt

DRESS:

Photos on pages 6-7.

Pattern Pieces:
TOP x1, BOTTOM x1, and STRAP x2

Supplies:
Sewing pattern basics (See pages 44-45)
Hook-and-loop closures
Rosette applique
Loop turner

Steps:
Before following the steps outlined in the diagram, cut enough of each pattern piece for this dress.

1. With right sides together, fold STRAP in half along the fold line and sew a seam. Using a loop turner, turn the strap inside out and press with the seam hidden in the middle of the backside. Repeat with other STRAP.

2. Fold over top of TOP piece and press with iron. Pin each strap on backside of TOP piece, where indicated. Double check strap length on doll. Top stitch to hold edge of TOP down and straps in place.

3. Fold over bottom of BOTTOM piece and top stitch.

4. On the BOTTOM piece, gather where indicated until gather is the length of the bottom of the TOP piece. With right sides together, pin gathered fabric to the TOP piece and sew a seam. Fold seam of BOTTOM and TOP pieces up and top stitch along the TOP piece of the dress.

5. Using a needle and thread, stitch rose applique in place on front of TOP piece in between the strap pieces.

6. With right sides together, sew seam from bottom of back of SKIRT up to ——O point on pattern. Turn inside out. See pages 47-50 for a hook-and-loop *Closures* guide.

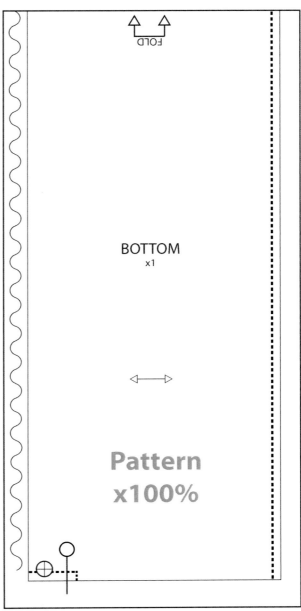

FOLD

BOTTOM
x1

Pattern x100%

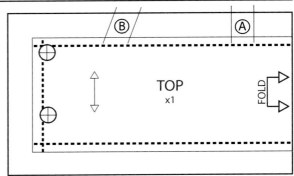

B   A

TOP
x1

FOLD

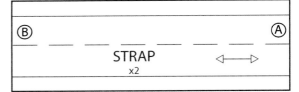

B   A

STRAP
x2

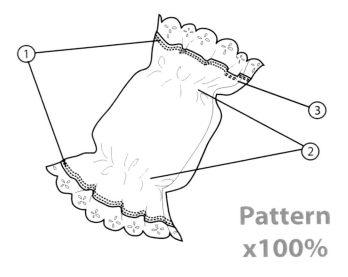

Pattern x100%

ARM SLEEVES:

Photos on pages 6-7.

Pattern Pieces:
SLEEVE x2

Supplies:
Sewing pattern basics (See pages 44-45)
Approximately 8 inches of elastic cording, 1/4 inch wide or less
Approximately 16 inches of lace trim

Steps:
Before following the steps outlined in the diagram, cut enough of each pattern piece for these arm sleeves. A lightweight fabric is recommended since the folded over fabric and elastic gathering may make the sleeve appear bulky.

1. Fold over top and bottom of SLEEVE. Press with iron. Measure out enough lace trim for the length of the top and bottom of the SLEEVE. Pin lace trim pieces on backside of SLEEVE top and bottom. Top stitch with two rows of stitches. Repeat for other SLEEVE.
2. Cut approximately 2 inches thin elastic. Where indicated on pattern to include elastic, baste stitch both ends of cording to either end of SLEEVE (inside the seam). While stretching the elastic, carefully top stitch to hold the elastic in place. A zigzag stitch can also be used for this step. Repeat this step for the other elastic indication on SLEEVE pattern. After one sleeve is done, repeat for other sleeve.
3. With right sides together, sew a seam of sides of each SLEEVE piece. Turn inside out.

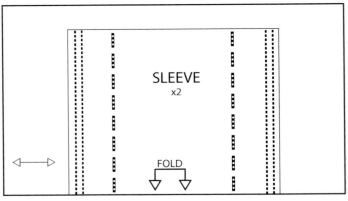

SLEEVE
x2

FOLD

Pattern Design
© 2014 MegannArt

APRON:

Photos on pages 4-5.

Pattern Pieces:
None required

Supplies:
Needle and thread
Approximately 16 inches of 3 mm, 6 mm, or other ribbon of similar width
Lace applique

Steps:
It may be difficult to find the perfect piece of applique for this apron. Sometimes trimming a section of a larger piece of applique may work well.

1. Before cutting your length of ribbon, test the length on the doll at the waist to ensure it will be easy to tie a bow in the back. Place center of applique behind ribbon center. Using a needle and thread, sew applique and ribbon together using a running stitch or similar stitch.

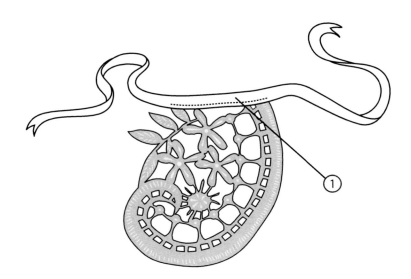

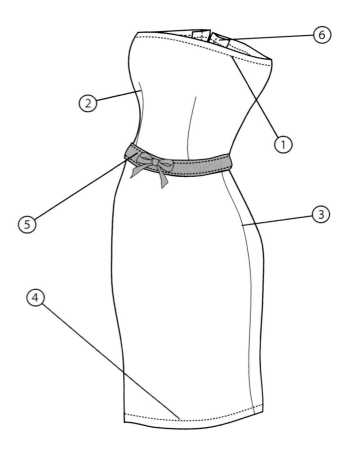

momoko

DRESS:

Photos on pages 10-11.

Pattern Pieces:
TOP x1, BACK x2, and FRONT x1

Supplies:
Sewing pattern basics (See pages 44-45)
Bead-and-loop closures
Approximately 8 inches of 3 mm wide ribbon

Steps:
Before following the steps outlined in the diagram, cut enough of each pattern piece for this dress.

1. Fold top of garment over and top stitch.
2. Make darts on either side of TOP piece by folding right side together and sewing along outer seams of dart. Repeat on other side of TOP piece. Press darts down center.
3. Sew seam of FRONT piece to a BACK piece with right sides together. Repeat with other BACK piece to other side of FRONT piece. Press seams.
4. Fold over bottom of skirt pieces and top stitch where indicated on pattern.
5. With right sides together, sew seam over top of skirt piece and bottom of TOP piece. Cut a piece of ribbon to fit entire length of seam. Fold seam of skirt and TOP pieces up and, with the ribbon pinned over the seam, top stitch along the ribbon. Two rows of stitches may be helpful and look best. Make a small bow with the 3 mm wide ribbon. Using a needle and thread, sew the bow to the center front of the ribbon belt.
6. With right sides together, sew seam from bottom of back of skirt up to ──o point on pattern. Turn inside out. See pages 47-50 for a bead-and-loop *Closures* guide.

Pattern x100%

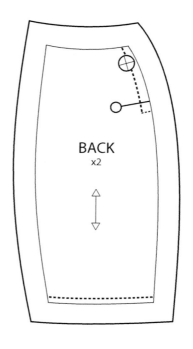

BACK
x2

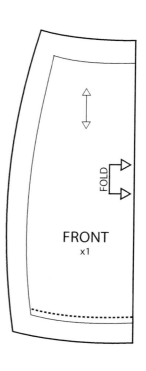

FOLD

FRONT
x1

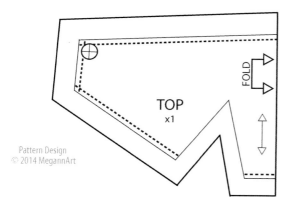

FOLD

TOP
x1

Pattern Design
© 2014 MegannArt

69

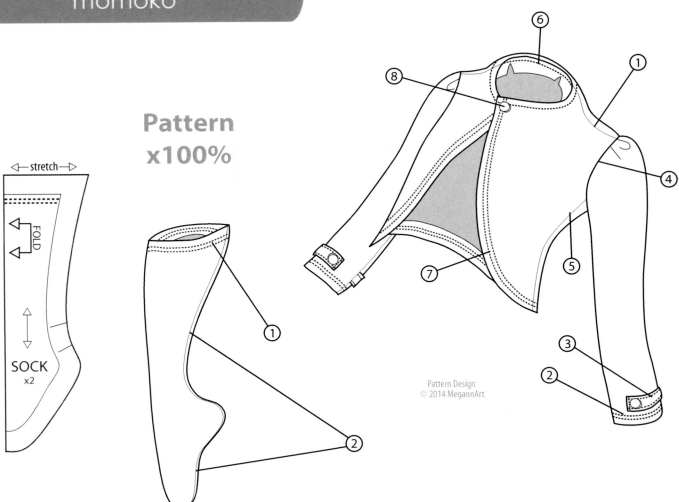

Pattern
x100%

←—stretch—→

FOLD

SOCK
x2

Pattern Design
© 2014 MegannArt

SOCKS:

Photos on pages 10-11.

Pattern Pieces:
SOCK x2

Supplies:
Sewing pattern basics (See pages 44-45)

Steps:
Before following the steps outlined in the diagram, cut enough of each pattern piece for these socks. Thin knit/stretchable fabric is required for this pattern.

1. Fold top side of the SOCK over and top stitch with two rows of stitches. Repeat for other SOCK piece.
2. With right sides together, sew seam from top of SOCK, down to the heel and through to the fold in the SOCK. Clip curves where indicated on pattern. Turn inside out and repeat for other SOCK piece.

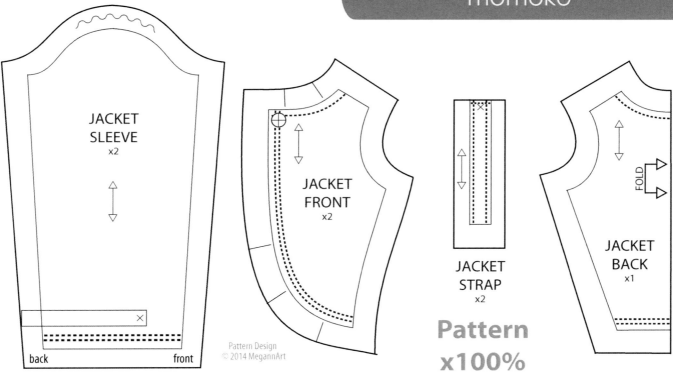

JACKET SLEEVE x2

JACKET FRONT x2

JACKET STRAP x2

JACKET BACK x1

FOLD

back   front

Pattern Design
© 2014 MegannArt

Pattern x100%

JACKET:

Photos on pages 10-11.

Pattern Pieces:
JACKET FRONT x2, JACKET BACK x1, JACKET SLEEVE x2, and JACKET STRAP x2

Supplies:
Sewing pattern basics (See pages 44-45)
Hook-and-eye closure
Tiny buttons or seed beads

Steps:
Before following the steps outlined in the diagram, cut enough of each pattern piece for this jacket.

1. With right sides togehter, sew shoulder seams of JACKET FRONT pieces to JACKET BACK. Press seams open.
2. Fold bottom side of the JACKET SLEEVE over and top stitch with two rows of stitches. Repeat for other JACKET SLEEVE.
3. Fold long edges of JACKET STRAP pieces back and press. Top stitch along both edges of JACKET STRAP pieces. Using a needle and thread, baste stitch the strap into the seam of the backside of the JACKET SLEEVE, where indicated on the pattern. Stitch the other end of the strap in place where indicated on the pattern. Using the needle and thread, stitch a button or bead where the "X" is on the pattern.
4. Make a small gather in area indicated on JACKET SLEEVE until length of sleeve is the same as the armhole opening. Ease upper JACKET SLEEVE into each armhole using sewing pins or basting stitch. Make sure right sides are together. Sew seam and repeat for other JACKET SLEEVE.
5. Sew seam from bottom of JACKET SLEEVE to armpit and then to the bottom of the garment. Clip curves, particularly at armpit area. Press seams from bottom of garment up to the armpit. Repeat on other side.
6. Clip curves of neck opening. Fold over neck opening and top stitch.
7. Clip curves of jacket opening. Fold over opening and pin in place or baste stitch. Top stitch with two rows of stitches.
8. Using a needle and thread, sew a button or bead on the garment where indicated with an "X". Hand sew hook-and-eye closure on the inside of the jacket where indicated on the pattern. See pages 47-50 for a helpful hook-and-eye *Closures* guide.

12 Inch Fashion Doll (FR)

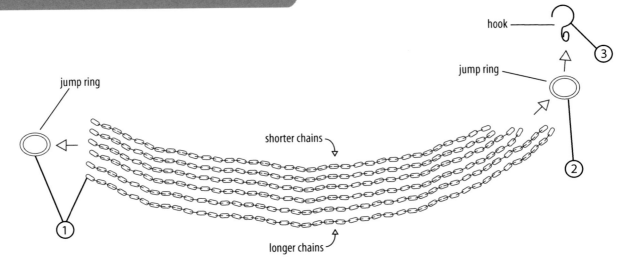

hook

jump ring ③

jump ring ②

jump ring ①

shorter chains

longer chains

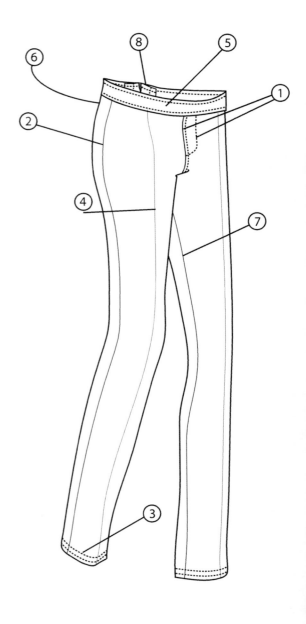

NECKLACE:

Photos on pages 8-9.

Supplies:
Lobster claw, hook, or other jewelry closure
Jewelry chain (approximately 24-3/4 inches)
Jump rings
Crimp pliers with cutter

Steps:
1. Cut six jewelry chains; two 4 inches in length, two 4-1/8 inches in length, and two 4-1/4 inches in length. Starting with the shortest chain lengths, place the end of each chain into the jump ring and close the jump ring shut.
2. Starting with the shortest chain length and ending with the longest chain length, place the end of each chain into the other jump ring.
3. Add the jewelry closure into the jump ring and close the jump ring shut.

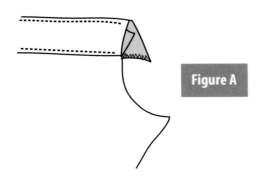

Figure A

SLACKS:

Photos on pages 8-9.

Pattern Pieces:
PANT FRONT x2, PANT BACK x2, and BELT x1

Supplies:
Sewing pattern basics (See pages 44-45)
Bead-and-loop closure

Steps:
Before following the steps outlined in the diagram, cut enough of each pattern piece for this pair of slacks. A lightweight fabric is recommended for this pattern.

BELT backside will have a raw edge. Sew an optional zigzag stitch along the backside, where indicated on pattern, if finished edge is desired. This optional step is not included in the directions below.

1. On left PANT FRONT piece, sew a decorative top stitch curve, as indicated on pattern. With right sides together, sew seam of rise in PANT FRONT pieces. Press open. Top stitch along seam line over left PANT FRONT piece.
2. With right sides together, sew seam of long length of corresponding PANT FRONT and PANT BACK pieces. Repeat with other side. Press seams open.
3. Turn bottom of pants under and top stitch with two rows of stitches.
4. Fold wrong sides of PANT FRONT piece together on indicated fold line, gently press front of PANT FRONT piece with iron. Iron well to create a fold in the slacks. Repeat with other PANT FRONT piece.
5. With right sides together, sew seam of top of pants to BELT. Fold BELT over seam (see Figure A) and top stitch along top and bottom of front side of belt.
6. With right sides together, sew seam of rise in PANT BACK pieces to —O point on pattern. Press seams open, if able.
7. With right sides together, sew seam from bottom of one pant leg, up to the rise, and down to the other pant leg. Clip curves, especially around the rise. Turn inside out. This is easier with hemostats.
8. See pages 47-50 for a bead-and-loop *Closures* guide.

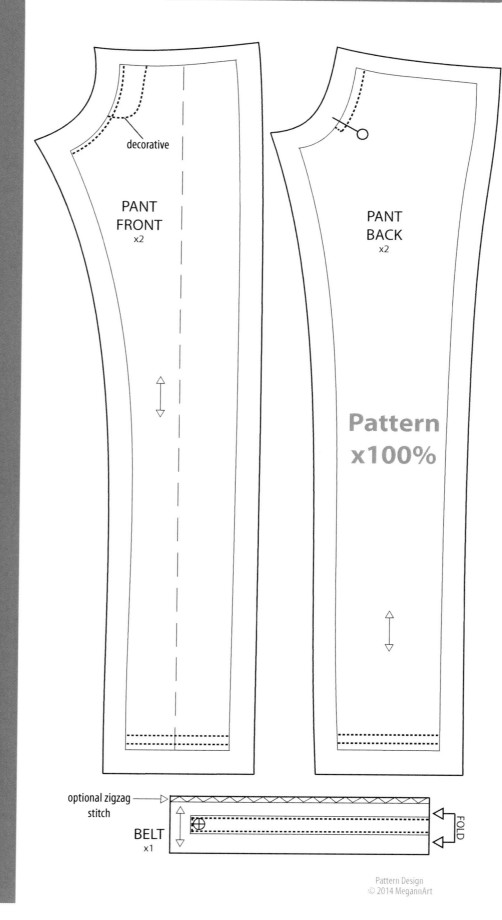

decorative

PANT FRONT x2

PANT BACK x2

Pattern x100%

optional zigzag stitch

BELT x1

FOLD

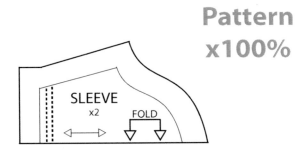

Pattern x100%

SLEEVE
x2

FOLD

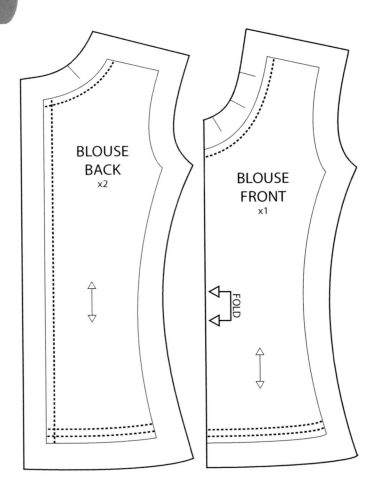

BLOUSE
BACK
x2

BLOUSE
FRONT
x1

FOLD

Pattern Design
© 2014 MegannArt

BLOUSE:

Photos on pages 8-9.

Pattern Pieces:
BLOUSE FRONT x1, BLOUSE BACK x2, and SLEEVE x2

Supplies:
Sewing pattern basics (See pages 44-45)
Hook-and-loop tape

Steps:
Before following the steps outlined in the diagram, cut enough of each pattern piece for this blouse.

1. Sew shoulder seams of BLOUSE FRONT to BLOUSE BACK pieces with the right sides together. Press seams open.
2. Clip edges of neck opening in the seam. Fold the neck opening over and baste stitch or pin in place. Top stitch folded edge.
3. Fold bottom side of each SLEEVE over and top stitch with two rows of stitches.
4. With right sides together, ease upper SLEEVE into each armhole using sewing pins or a basting stitch. Sew seam and repeat for other SLEEVE.
5. With right sides together, sew seam from opening of SLEEVE to armpit and then to the bottom of the garment. Clip curves, especially under armpit. Repeat on other side. Press seams from bottom of garment to armpit area.
6. Fold over bottom opening of garment and top stitch with two rows of stitches.
7. Fold over open edge of back pieces and sew hook-and-loop tape into back of garment. See pages 47-50 for a hook-and-loop *Closures* guide.

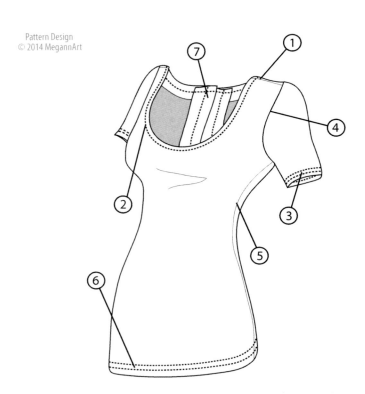

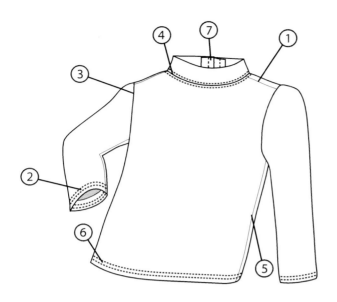

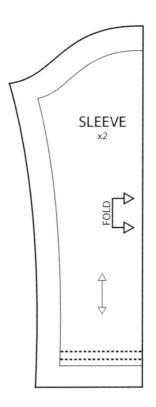

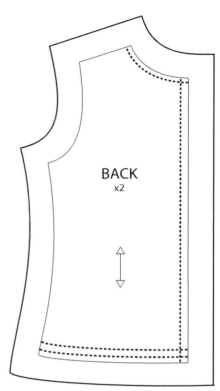

TURTLENECK:

Photos on pages 22, 23 and cover.

Pattern Pieces:
FRONT x1, BACK x2, SLEEVE x2, and COLLAR x1

Supplies:
Sewing pattern basics (See pages 44-45)
Hook-and-loop closure tape

Steps:
Before following the steps outlined in the diagram, cut enough of each pattern piece for this turtleneck. A knit/stretchable fabric is recommended.

1. Sew shoulder seams of FRONT to BACK pieces with the right sides together. Press seams open.
2. Fold bottom side of each SLEEVE over and top stitch with two rows of stitches.
3. Ease upper SLEEVE into each armhole using sewing pins or a basting stitch. Make sure right sides are together. Sew seam and repeat for other SLEEVE.
4. Fold COLLAR in half the long way, making sure to expose the right side of the fabric. Press the fold. With right sides together, sew seam of folded collar to neck opening. Press seams open. Top stitch over both sides of the seam.
5. With right sides together, sew seam from bottom of SLEEVE to armpit and then to the bottom of the garment. Clip curves, especially under armpit. Repeat on other side.
6. Fold over bottom of sweater and top stitch with two rows of stitches.
7. Fold over open edge of back pieces and sew hook-and-loop tape into back of garment. See pages 47-50 for a helpful hook-and-loop *Closures* guide.

Pattern Design
© 2014 MegannArt

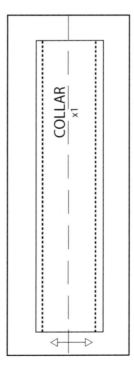

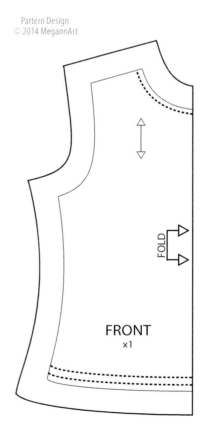

Pattern x100%

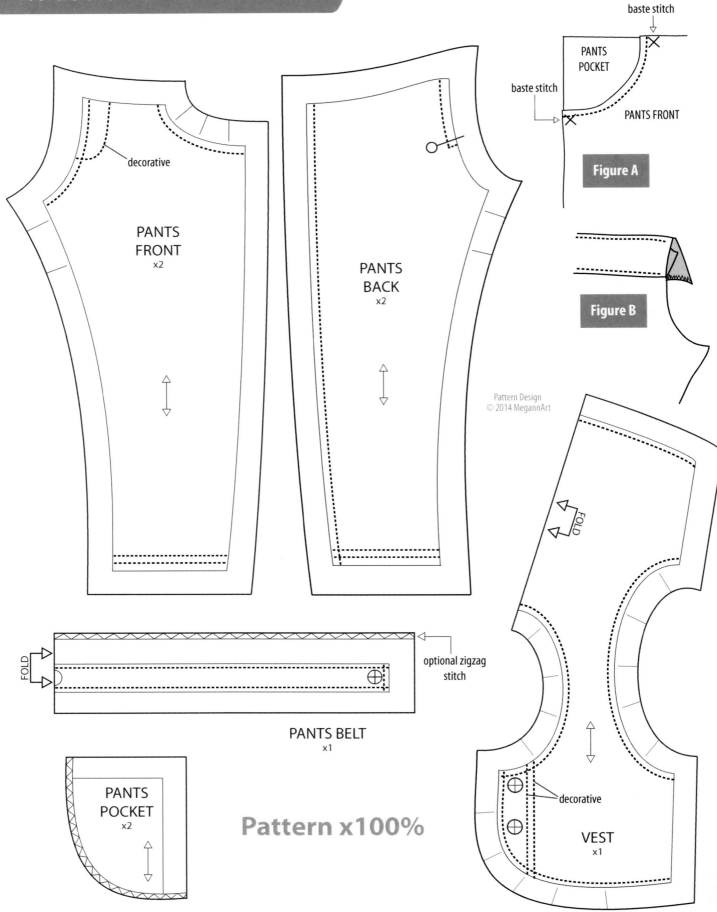

baste stitch

PANTS POCKET

baste stitch

PANTS FRONT

Figure A

Figure B

decorative

PANTS FRONT
x2

PANTS BACK
x2

Pattern Design
© 2014 MegannArt

FOLD

FOLD

optional zigzag stitch

PANTS BELT
x1

PANTS POCKET
x2

Pattern x100%

decorative

VEST
x1

PANTS:

Photos on pages 22, 23 and cover.

Pattern Pieces:
PANTS FRONT x2, PANTS BACK x2, PANTS POCKET x2, and PANTS BELT x1

Supplies:
Sewing pattern basics (See pages 44-45)
Button, rivet, or iron/glue-on metal applique
Bead-and-loop closure

Steps:
Before following the steps outlined in the diagram, cut enough of each pattern piece for this pair of slacks.

BELT backside will have a raw edge. Sew an optional zigzag stitch along the backside, where indicated on pattern, if finished edge is desired. This optional step is not included in the directions below.

1. Clip curves of pockets opening on PANTS FRONT pieces. Fold pocket openings over and pin in place or baste stitch. Top stitch.
2. On left PANTS FRONT piece, sew a decorative top stitch curve, as indicated on pattern. With right sides together, sew seam of rise in PANTS FRONT pieces. Press open. Top stitch along seam line over left PANTS FRONT piece.
3. With right side of pocket facing wrong side of PANTS FRONT piece, baste stitch the pocket in place in the seam (see Figure A).
4. With right sides together, sew seam of long length of corresponding PANTS FRONT and PANTS BACK pieces. Press seams open. Top stitch on the PANTS BACK piece. Repeat with other side.
5. Turn bottom of pants under and top stitch with two rows of stitches.
6. With right sides together, sew seam of top of pants to PANTS BELT. Fold PANTS BELT over seam (see Figure B) and top stitch along top and bottom of front side of belt.
7. With right sides together, sew seam of rise in PANTS BACK pieces to ——O point on pattern. Press seams open, if able.
8. With right sides together, sew seam from bottom of one pant leg, up to the rise, and down to the other pant leg. Clip curves at rise. Turn inside out. Hemostats are helpful for turning pants inside out.
9. See pages 47-50 for a bead-and-loop *Closures* guide.

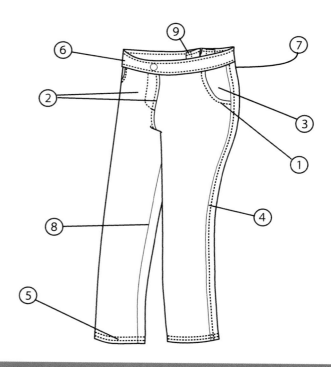

VEST:

Photos on pages 22, 23 and cover.

Pattern Pieces:
VEST x1

Supplies:
Sewing pattern basics (See pages 44-45)
Tiny buttons or seed beads
Hook-and-eye closures

Steps:
Before following the steps outlined in the diagram, cut the pattern piece for this vest.

1. Clip curves of neck opening. Fold neck opening over and pin in place or baste stitch. Top stitch.
2. Clip curves of arm openings. Fold arm openings over and pin in place or baste stitch. Top stitch.
3. With right sides together, sew seam from bottom of VEST to armpit. Repeat on other side. Press seams open.
4. Clip curves on bottom of vest. Fold raw edges over and pin in place or baste stitch. Top stitch starting from one side of opening, along bottom edge, and up to the other side of opening.
5. Top stitch two rows of decorative stitches vertically along right opening of the vest.
6. Using a needle and thread, sew tiny buttons or seed beads along the left opening of the vest. Attach hook-and-eye closures to the vest where indicated on pattern. See pages 47-50 for a helpful *Closures* guide on using hook-and-eye closures.

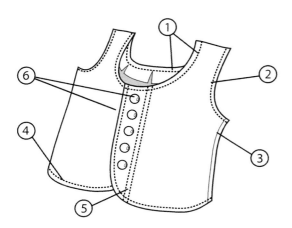

77

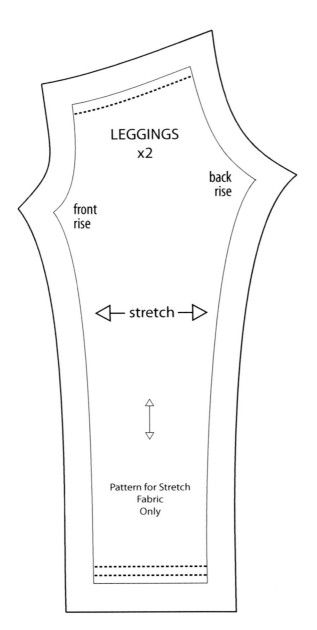

LEGGINGS
x2

back
rise

front
rise

←— stretch —→

Pattern for Stretch
Fabric
Only

Pattern
x100%

Pattern Design
© 2014 MegannArt

LEGGINGS:

Photo on page 12.

Pattern Pieces:
LEGGINGS x2

Supplies:
Sewing pattern basics (See pages 44-45)

Steps:
Before following the steps outlined in the diagram, cut enough of each pattern piece for these leggings. The pattern is specifically meant for knit/stretch fabric.

1. With right sides together of both LEGGINGS pieces, sew seam of front rise. If fabric is iron-friendly, press seams open.
2. Fold top of leggings over and top stitch.
3. Fold the bottom side of each pant leg over and top stitch with two rows of stitches.
4. With right sides together of both LEGGINGS pieces, sew seam of back rise.
5. With right sides together, sew seam from bottom of one pant leg up to the rise and then down the other pant leg. Clip curves at rise. Turn inside out.

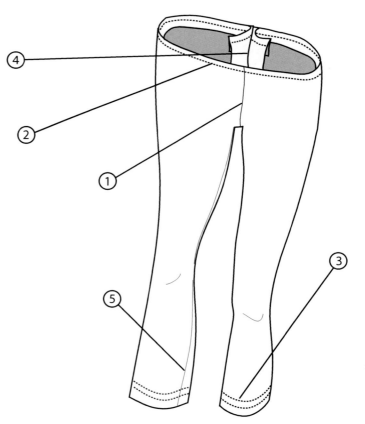

Pattern Design
© 2014 MegannArt

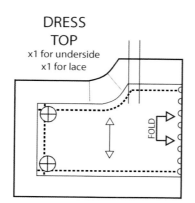

DRESS
TOP
x1 for underside
x1 for lace

FOLD

Pattern
x100%

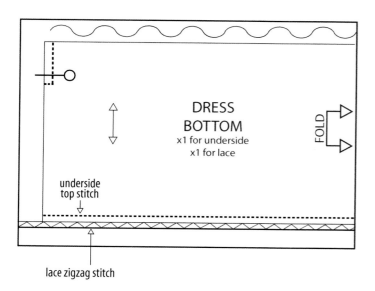

DRESS
BOTTOM
x1 for underside
x1 for lace

FOLD

underside
top stitch

lace zigzag stitch

DRESS:

Photo on page 12.

Pattern Pieces:
DRESS TOP x1 for lace and x1 for underside, DRESS BOTTOM x1 for lace and x1 for underside

Supplies:
Sewing pattern basics (See pages 44-45)
Approximately 8 inches of cording, twine, or 3mm wide ribbon
Tiny buttons or seed beads
Bead-and-loop closures

Steps:
Before following the steps outlined in the diagram, cut enough of each pattern piece for this dress. Lace fabric was used as the outside layer of the entire dress. There is some stretch in the fabrics used for this pattern.

1. Clip curves of lace and underside fabrics on DRESS TOP. With lace fabric on front side of underside fabric, fold over top and pin in place or baste stitch. Where indicated on pattern, attach 4 inches of cording, ribbon, or twine to back of both sides of DRESS TOP with a temporary baste stitch or pin. Top stitch to hold fabric and straps in place.
2. Fold over bottom of underside DRESS BOTTOM and top stitch.
3. Sew a zigzag stitch along bottom of DRESS BOTTOM lace fabric. Trim excess lace fabric for a clean edge.
4. With lace fabric on front side of underside fabric, gather top of DRESS BOTTOM pieces until they are the length of the bottom of the DRESS TOP pieces. With right sides together, sew seam over skirt pieces and top pieces.
5. Fold seam of skirt and top pieces up and top stitch along the DRESS TOP pieces.
6. With right sides together, sew seam from bottom of dress to ——o point on pattern. Turn inside out. See pages 47-50 for a bead-and-loop *Closures* guide. Hand-sewing this step may be helpful since the dress is very small.
7. Using a needle and thread, attach tiny buttons or seed beads along the center front of the DRESS TOP piece.

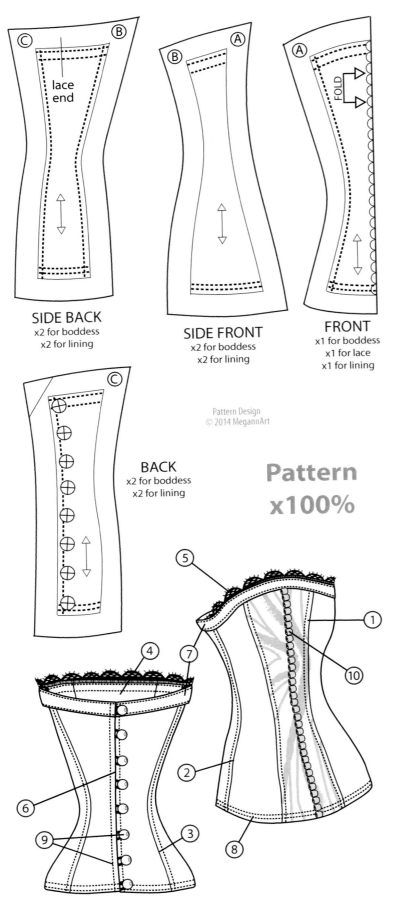

C B

lace
end

SIDE BACK
x2 for boddess
x2 for lining

B A

SIDE FRONT
x2 for boddess
x2 for lining

A

FOLD

FRONT
x1 for boddess
x1 for lace
x1 for lining

C

BACK
x2 for boddess
x2 for lining

Pattern Design
© 2014 MegannArt

Pattern x100%

BODICE:

Photos on pages 4-5.

Pattern Pieces:
FRONT x1 for bodice, lace, and lining, SIDE FRONT x2 for bodice and lining, SIDE BACK x2 for bodice and lining, and BACK x2 for bodice and lining

Supplies:
Sewing pattern basics (See pages 44-45)
Ribbon (1/4 inch wide)
Lace trim
Bead-and-loop closures

Steps:
Before following the steps outlined in the diagram, cut enough of each pattern piece for this bodice. Lightweight fabric is recommended for the bodice and lining of this pattern.

1. With wrong side of FRONT lace piece on right side of the bodice FRONT pieces, sew a seam down FRONT and SIDE FRONT pieces on the seam side marked "A". Press seams open. Top stitch seam on both sides of FRONT pieces.
2. Sew a seam down the SIDE FRONT and SIDE BACK pieces on the seam side marked "B". Press seams. Top stitch along the SIDE BACK pieces.
3. Sew a seam down the SIDE BACK and BACK pieces on the seam side marked "C". Press seams. Top stitch along the SIDE BACK pieces.
4. Repeat the first three steps for the lining. Omit the lace FRONT piece for lining.
5. Cut a piece of lace trim approximately 4 inches long. Find center of top of FRONT and lace trim. With right sides together, baste stitch lace trim into seam. Taper lace into bodice at "lace end" on SIDE BACK pieces. With right sides together, sew a seam along top of lining and top of bodice.
6. Sew seam along lining BACK and bodice BACK pieces. Repeat for other side. Clip top corners. Turn inside out and press. Optional: For a cleaner look of the fasteners, put loop portion of fasteners in between bodice and lining before sewing the seam. However, this is optional and loops can be placed during step 9.
7. Cut enough 1/4 wide ribbon for the length of the top of bodice. Place ribbon along top of lace trim and bodice with pins or a baste stitch. Top stitch along top and bottom of ribbon to hold it in place.
8. Turn bottom of bodice and lining in and press. Top stitch two rows of stitches.
9. Top stitch along seam on both sides of back opening of bodice. Using a needle and thread, sew several bead-and-loop closures into the back of the bodice. See pages 47-50 for a helpful bead-and-loop *Closures* guide.
10. Using a needle and thread, attach seed beads up the center front of the FRONT piece.

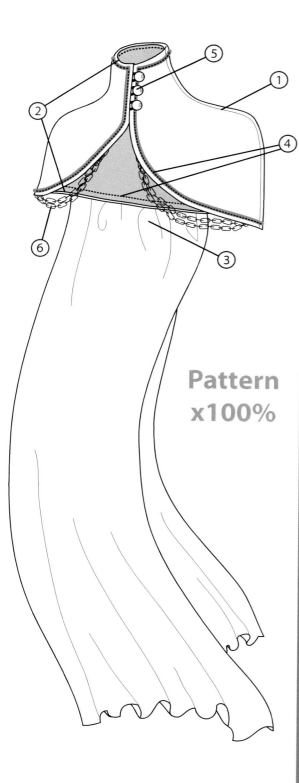

Pattern x100%

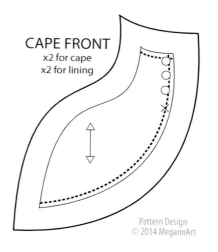

CAPE FRONT
x2 for cape
x2 for lining

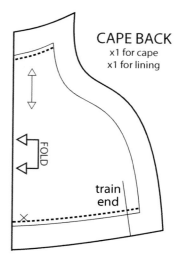

CAPE BACK
x1 for cape
x1 for lining

FOLD

train end

Pattern Design
© 2014 MegannArt

Figure A

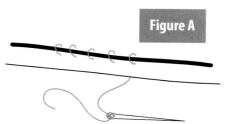

CAPE:

Photos on pages 4-5.

Pattern Pieces:
CAPE FRONT x2 for cape and lining and CAPE BACK x1 for cape and lining

Supplies:
Sewing pattern basics (See pages 44-45)
Bead-and-loop closures
Twine, embroidery thread, or similar item
Jewelry chain
Jewelry cutter for chain
Two tulle pieces for train (measurements: 8-1/2 x 18 inches and 11 x 18 inches)

Steps:
Before following the steps outlined in the diagram, cut enough of each pattern piece for this cape. Lightweight iron-friendly fabric is recommended for the cape and lining of this pattern.

1. With right sides together, sew a seam down the side of the CAPE BACK to a CAPE FRONT piece. Repeat with other side of CAPE BACK to other CAPE FRONT piece. Press seams open. Repeat this step for the lining pieces.
2. With right sides together of the lining and cape garments, sew a seam from the back of the cape where marked "train end", up the front, around the neck opening, down the other front side, then to the other "train end". A small section in the back of the garment should be left open. Turn inside out and press seam.
3. Gather both pieces of tulle on the 18-inch side until the gather measures the length of the back opening left in cape. Place gathered fabric inside cape about 1/4 inches, with the shorter of the two tulle pieces on the cape side and the longer on the lining side. Fold remaining CAPE BACK lining and cape in and baste stitch in place, also holding the gathered tulle in place.
4. Top stitch over entire opening of garment, starting in the back. Attach twine with needle and thread (see Figure A) directly over top stitch.
5. Attach bead-and-loop closures to cape, where indicated. See pages 47-50 for a helpful bead-and-loop *Closures* guide.
6. Cut two pieces of chain 3 inches long and two pieces of chain 3-1/8 inches long. Using a needle and thread, sew one end of a 3 inch and 3-1/8 chain to "X" on backside of CAPE FRONT. Hand sew the other ends of two chains to "X" on backside of CAPE BACK. Repeat with other two chains to other CAPE FRONT and CAPE BACK sides.

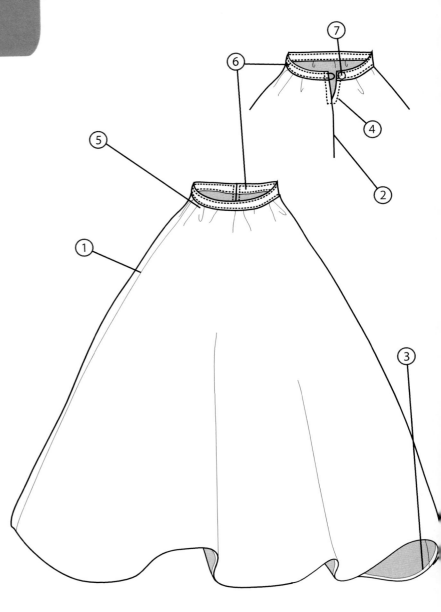

12 Inch Fashion Doll (FR)

SKIRT:

Photos on pages 4-5.

Pattern Pieces:
SKIRT FRONT x1 for skirt and lining, SKIRT BACK x2 for skirt and lining, and SKIRT BELT x1

Supplies:
Sewing pattern basics (See pages 44-45)
Bead-and-loop closure

Steps:
Before following the steps outlined in the diagram, cut enough of each pattern piece for this skirt. Lightweight iron-friendly fabric is recommended for the skirt and lining of this pattern. It is not recommended to replace the fastener with an overlapping snap or other similar closure since the skirt will be tight under the boddess.

1. With right sides together, sew a seam down the side of the SKIRT FRONT to a SKIRT BACK piece. Repeat with other side of SKIRT FRONT to other SKIRT BACK piece. Press seams open. Repeat this step for the lining pieces.
2. With right sides together, sew a seam from the bottom of the skirt up to the O—— point on the pattern. Press seam open. Repeat this step for the lining.
3. With right sides together, sew a seam joining the skirt and lining along the bottom opening. Turn inside out and press with skirt folding inside the garment about 1/16 inch (approximately 2 mm). This will prevent the lining from being visible when resting on the doll.
4. Turn closure opening of skirt and lining in and baste stitch or pin in place. Top stitch over skirt and lining from the top of one SKIRT BACK piece, down and over the seam, and then up and over the other SKIRT BACK piece. Optional: For a cleaner look, sew the loop part of the bead-and-loop closure into the seam during this step to have the loop hidden. However, this is optional and a bead-and-loop closure can be finished at the end, during step 7.
5. Gather the opening of the skirt until it is the same length of the SKIRT BELT piece. With right side of skirt and SKIRT BELT together, pin gathered fabric every 1/2 to inch to the SKIRT BELT. Sew a seam.
6. Fold short edges of SKIRT BELT in. Fold long raw edge of SKIRT BELT in to close off all raw edges of SKIRT BELT. Press. Fold SKIRT BELT over seam. Top stitch around front side of the SKIRT BELT (see Figure A).
7. See pages 47-50 for a bead-and-loop *Closures* guide.

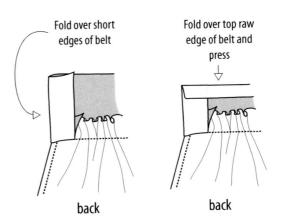

Fold over short edges of belt

back

Fold over top raw edge of belt and press

back

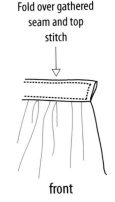

Fold over gathered seam and top stitch

front

Figure A

82

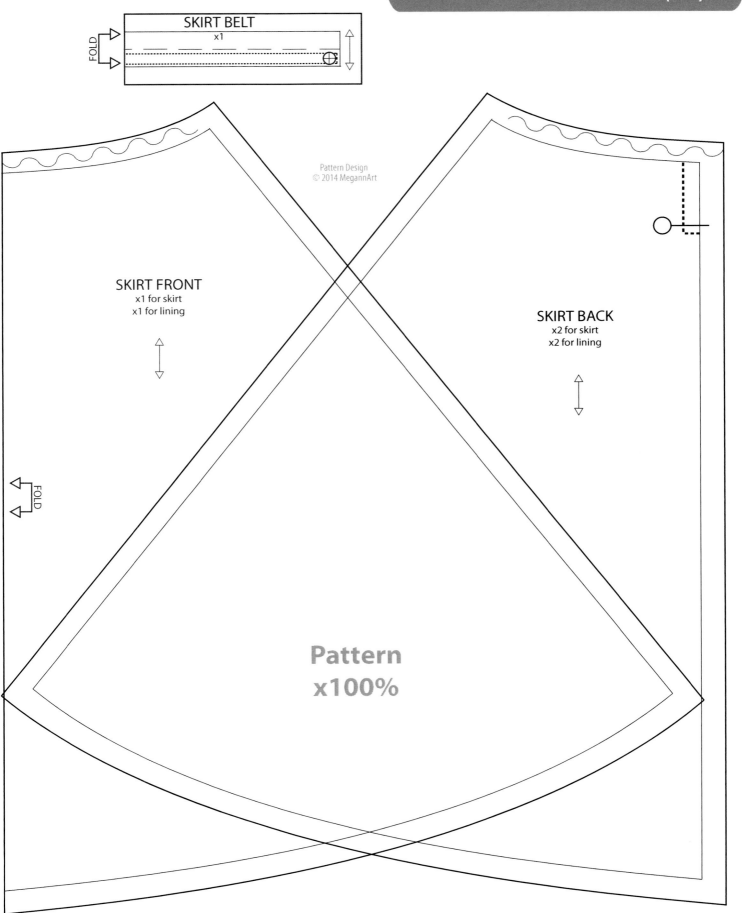

SKIRT BELT
x1

FOLD

SKIRT FRONT
x1 for skirt
x1 for lining

SKIRT BACK
x2 for skirt
x2 for lining

Pattern Design
© 2014 MegannArt

FOLD

Pattern
x100%

Super Slim 10.5 Inch Dolls

TOP:

Photo on page 17.

Pattern Pieces:
TOP x1

Supplies:
Sewing pattern basics (See pages 44-45)
Approximately 4 inches of 3 mm wide ribbon, plus more to make a tiny bow
Three tiny buttons or seed beads
Hook-and-loop tape

Steps:
Before following the steps outlined in the diagram, cut he pattern piece for this top.

1. Clip curves where indicated on the TOP. Fold over top opening of TOP and pin in place or baste stitch. Cut two pieces of 3 mm wide ribbon 2 inches in length. Where indicated on pattern, attach one piece of ribbon to section marked "A" with a temporary baste stitch or pin. The ribbon should be about 1/4 inch into the seam. Take the other end of the ribbon and attach to section marked "B" with a temporary baste stitch or pin. Repeat with other side of top and other ribbon piece. Double check strap length by testing it on doll. Top stitch over entire folded edge, being sure that the stitch holds straps in place.
2. Fold over bottom edge of top and press. Top stitch with two rows of stitches.
3. Add hook-and-loop tape to the back of the TOP. See pages 47-50 for a helpful hook-and-loop *Closures* guide.
4. Make a bow with ribbon. Using a needle and thread, attach a bow and tiny buttons or seed beads.

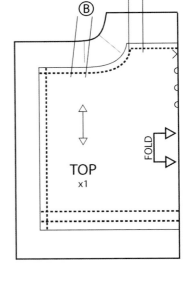

Pattern x100%

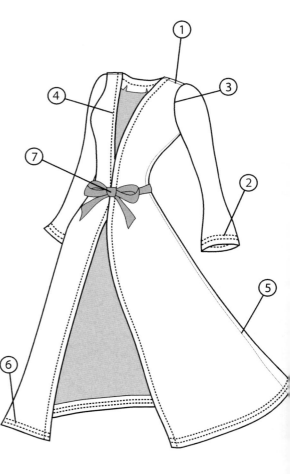

Pattern Design
© 2014 MegannArt

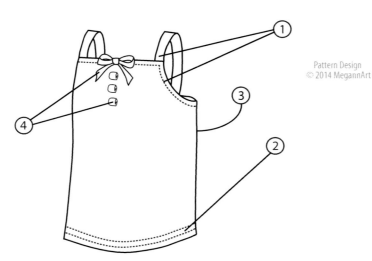

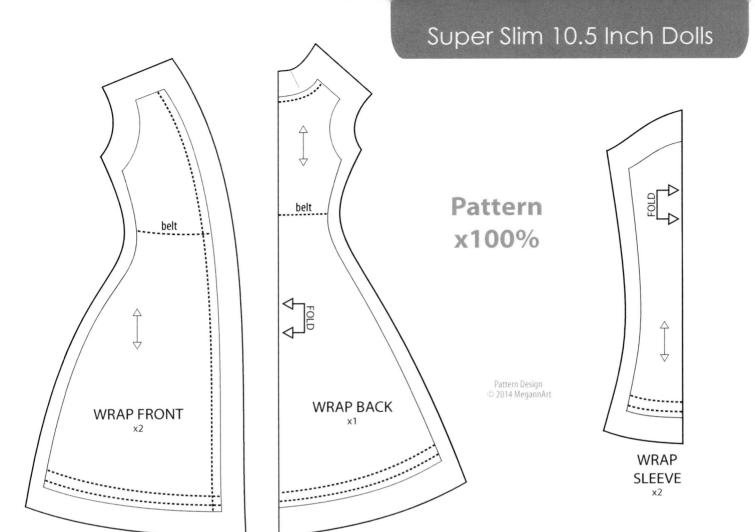

WRAP FRONT
x2

WRAP BACK
x1

belt

FOLD

Pattern x100%

Pattern Design
© 2014 MegannArt

WRAP SLEEVE
x2

FOLD

WRAP:

Photo on page 17.

Pattern Pieces:
WRAP FRONT x2, WRAP BACK x1, and WRAP SLEEVE x2

Supplies:
Sewing pattern basics (See pages 44-45)
Approximately 12 inches of 3 mm wide ribbon

Steps:
Before following the steps outlined in the diagram, cut enough of each pattern piece for this long wrap. Jersey fabric was used for this pattern.

1. Sew shoulder seams of WRAP FRONT pieces to WRAP BACK with the right sides together. Press seams open.
2. Fold bottom side of the WRAP SLEEVE over and top stitch with two rows of stitches. Repeat for other WRAP SLEEVE.
3. Ease upper WRAP SLEEVE into armhole using sewing pins or basting stitch. Make sure right sides are together. Sew seam and repeat for other WRAP SLEEVE.
4. Clip curves around neck opening. Fold over front/neck opening of wrap and top stitch.
5. Sew seam from opening of WRAP SLEEVE to armpit and then to the bottom of the wrap, joining the WRAP FRONT and WRAP BACK pieces. Clip curves, especially at armpit area. Repeat on other side. Press seams open from bottom of garment to armpit.
6. Fold over remaining open edge of wrap bottom and top stitch with two rows of stitches. Press, if necessary.
7. Top stitch ribbon along "belt" line indicated on pattern. Make sure slack is equal on both sides of wrap opening. When dressing doll, tie a bow in the front.

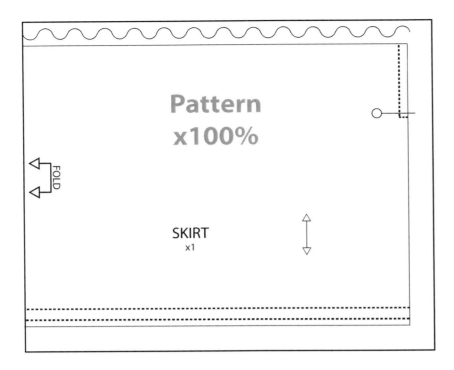

Pattern x100%

FOLD

SKIRT
x1

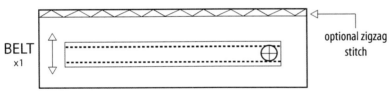

BELT
x1

optional zigzag stitch

Pattern Design
© 2014 MegannArt

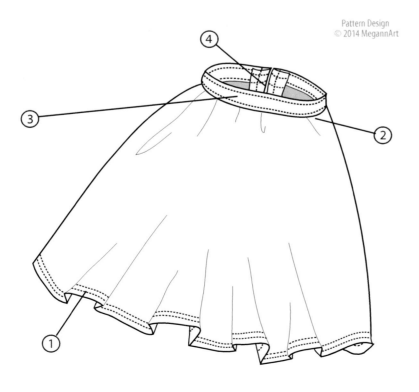

SKIRT:

Photo on page 17.

Pattern Pieces:
SKIRT x1 and BELT x1

Supplies:
Sewing pattern basics (See pages 44-45)
Bead-and-loop closure

Steps:
Before following the steps outlined in the diagram, cut enough of each pattern piece for this skirt. BELT backside will have a raw edge. Sew an optional zigzag stitch along the backside, where indicated on pattern, if finished edge is desired. This optional step is not included in the directions below.

1. Fold bottom side of SKIRT over and top stitch with two rows of stitches.
2. On the SKIRT, gather where indicated until gather is the length of the BELT. With right sides together, pin gathered fabric every 1/2 inch to inch to the BELT. Sew seam.
3. Fold BELT over seam and top stitch along top and bottom of front side of belt (see Figure A).
4. With right sides together, sew seam from bottom of back of SKIRT up to o—— point on pattern. Hand-stitching the remaining part of the closure step may be helpful since the skirt is very small. Turn inside out. See pages 47-50 for a bead-and-loop *Closures* guide.

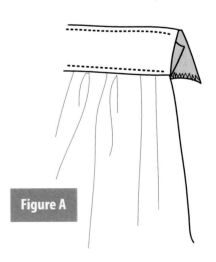

Figure A

DRESS:

Photo on page 3.

Pattern Pieces:
TOP x1 and BOTTOM x1

Supplies:
Sewing pattern basics (See pages 44-45)
Lace trim
Ribbon (1/4 inch wide and 3 mm wide)

Steps:
Before following the steps outlined in the diagram, cut enough of each pattern piece for this halter dress. Lightweight iron-friendly fabric is recommended for the dress.

1. Cut enough lace for the length of the long side of the BOTTOM piece. Fold bottom side of BOTTOM piece over and press. Pin lace to the back of the pressed fabric. Top stitch with two rows of stitches. Lace should be held in place with the top stitch.
2. Fold over both short sides of BOTTOM piece and press. Top stitch with two rows of stitches.
3. Fold over sides and top of TOP piece and pin in place or baste stitch. Ironing fabric to hold in place may be helpful. Where indicated on pattern, attach approximately 4 inches of 3 mm wide ribbon to back of both sides of TOP with a temporary baste stitch or pin. Top stitch to hold fabric and straps in place.
4. On the BOTTOM, gather where indicated until the gather length is about 2-1/4 inches. Cut approximately 9-3/4 inches of 1/4 wide ribbon and find center. Find center of gathered BOTTOM piece and pin right side to center of wrong side of ribbon center. Pin gathered fabric every 1/2 inch to inch to the ribbon. Find center of bottom of TOP piece and pin right side to wrong side of ribbon center. Sew seam along top and bottom of ribbon to hold TOP and BOTTOM pieces to ribbon.

Super Tiny BJD (10-12 cm)

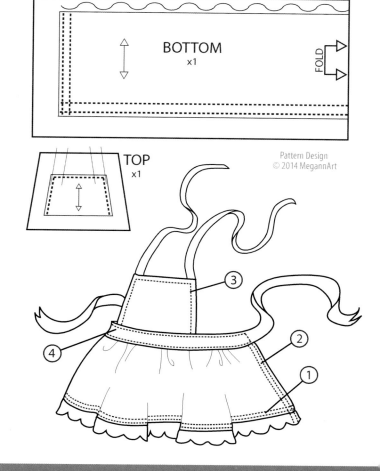

Pattern Design
© 2014 MegannArt

Pattern x100%

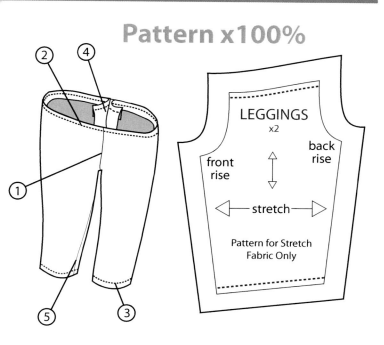

LEGGINGS:

Photos on pages 2-3.

Pattern Pieces:
LEGGINGS x2

Supplies:
Sewing pattern basics (See pages 44-45)

Steps:
Before following the steps outlined in the diagram, cut enough of the pattern piece for these leggings. The pattern is specifically meant for knit/stretch fabric.

1. With right sides together of both LEGGINGS pieces, sew seam of front rise. If fabric is iron-friendly, press seams open.
2. Fold top of leggings over and top stitch.
3. Fold the bottom side of each pant leg over and top stitch.
4. With right sides together of both LEGGINGS pieces, sew seam of back rise.
5. With right sides together, sew seam from bottom of one pant leg up to the rise and then down the other pant leg. Turn inside out.

JACKET:

Photo on page 2.

Pattern Pieces:
HOOD OUTSIDE x2, HOOD LINING x2, EARS x2 for inside and x2 for outside, JACKET BACK x1, JACKET FRONT x2, and SLEEVE x2

Supplies:
Sewing pattern basics (See pages 44-45)
Tiny buttons or seed beads
Twine or crochet thread

Steps:
Before following the steps outlined in the diagram, cut enough of each pattern piece for this hooded jacket. Lightweight iron-friendly fabric is recommended.

1. Sew shoulder seams of JACKET FRONT to JACKET BACK with the right sides together. Press seams open.

2. Fold bottom side of each SLEEVE over and top stitch with two rows of stitches.

3. Ease upper SLEEVE into each armhole using sewing pins or basting stitch. Make sure right sides are together. Sew seam and repeat for other SLEEVE.

4. With right sides together, sew seam from opening of SLEEVE to armpit and then to the bottom of the garment. Clip curves, especially under armpit. Repeat on other side.

5. With right sides together, sew seam around an inside and outside EARS piece. Leave bottom of ears open. Clip top point of ears and clip curves. Turn inside out and press. Repeat for other EARS inside/outside pieces. Pinch bottom of ears in half and place inside right side of dart on HOOD OUTSIDE pieces. Sew dart seam. Press seams of dart open, if able.

6. With right sides together, sew seam along curved edges of HOOD OUTSIDE pieces. Clip curves and press seams open. Repeat steps for HOOD LINING pieces.

7. With right sides together, sew seam of front opening of HOOD LINING to front opening of HOOD OUTSIDE pieces. Turn inside out and press seams.

8. With backside of hood (HOOD OUTSIDE pieces) to right side of neck opening of jacket, sew a seam. Make sure hood is in center of neck opening before sewing the seam. Fold hood down and top stitch over neck opening.

9. Fold over remaining raw edge of jacket and top stitch from bottom backside of jacket to the front opening, up to the neck opening, around the hood, down to other side of jacket opening, and meet first stitch on the backside of the jacket.

10. Sew an additional top stitch on the inside of the first stitch, starting from the neck opening, down the jacket opening, to the back of the jacket, and around the side to the other neck opening. The second row of stitches does not go over the hood.

11. Where indicated on pattern, sew tiny buttons or beads to the front opening. Repeat this step for loops on the other side of the jacket. See pages 47-50 for a helpful *Closures* guide on using bead-and-loop closures.

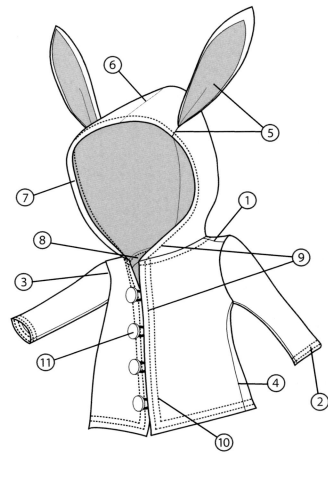

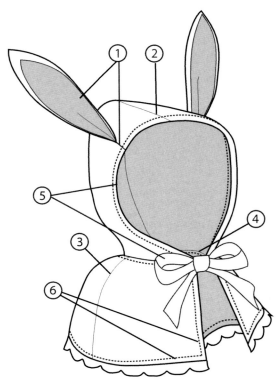

CAPE:

Photo on page 3.

Pattern Pieces:
HOOD OUTSIDE x2, HOOD LINING x2, EARS x2 for inside and x2 for outside, CAPE BACK x1 for inside and x1 for outside, and CAPE FRONT x2 for inside and x2 for outside

Supplies:
Sewing pattern basics (See pages 44-45)
Lace trim
Ribbon (1/4 inch wide)

Steps:
Before following the steps outlined in the diagram, cut enough of each pattern piece for this hooded cape. Lightweight iron-friendly fabric is recommended.

1. With right sides together, sew seam around an inside and outside EARS piece. Leave bottom of ears open. Clip top point of ears and clip curves. Turn inside out and press. Repeat for other EARS inside/outside pieces. Pinch bottom of ears in half and place inside right side of dart on HOOD OUTSIDE pieces. Sew dart seam. Press seams of dart open, if able.
2. With right sides together, sew seam along curved edges of HOOD OUTSIDE pieces. Clip curves and press seams open. Repeat steps for HOOD LINING pieces.
3. With right sides together, sew CAPE BACK curved (shoulder) side to a CAPE FRONT curved (shoulder) side of outside pieces. Repeat with other side of CAPE BACK and other CAPE FRONT piece. Clip curves and press seams open. Repeat steps for CAPE BACK and CAPE FRONT inside pieces.
4. With right sides together, sew neck opening of cape inside pieces to HOOD LINING pieces. Turn seams down onto the cape and top stitch. With right sides together, sew outside cape neck opening to HOOD OUTSIDE pieces. Turn seams down onto the cape and top stitch.
5. Cut 2 pieces of approximately 4-5 inches of 1/4-inch wide ribbon. Cut more if larger bow is desired. Where indicated on pattern, pin each ribbon to CAPE FRONT pieces. The long length of the ribbon should be inside the cape during this step and a small portion of ribbon into the seam. With right sides together, sew seam of cape inside/lining pieces to outside pieces from bottom of cape opening, up over the hood, and down to the other side of the cape opening. Turn inside out and press seams.
6. Cut enough lace trim for the length of the bottom of the cape (approximately 4-1/4 inches). Turn edges of bottom of cape in and insert lace in between inside and outside pieces. Pin or baste stitch in place. Top stitch from bottom of cape to the opening, over the opening of the hood, and back down the other side of cape opening and bottom. Top stitch should hold lace in place.

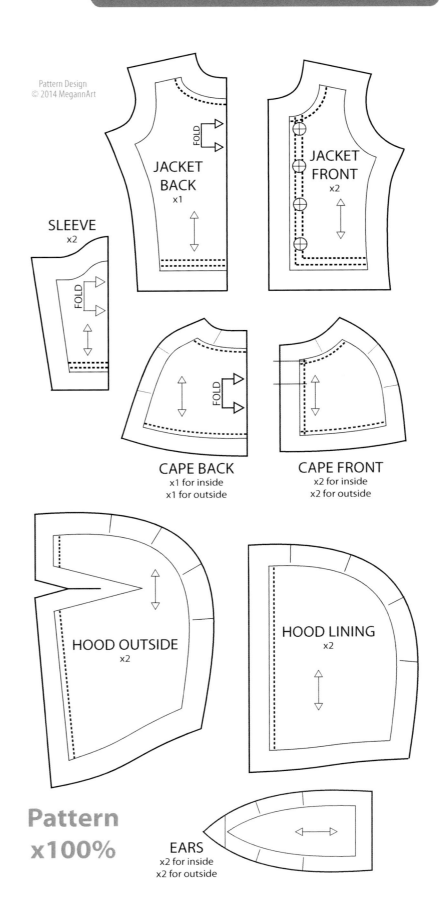

Pattern Design
© 2014 MegannArt

SLEEVE
x2

JACKET
BACK
x1

JACKET
FRONT
x2

CAPE BACK
x1 for inside
x1 for outside

CAPE FRONT
x2 for inside
x2 for outside

HOOD OUTSIDE
x2

HOOD LINING
x2

Pattern x100%

EARS
x2 for inside
x2 for outside

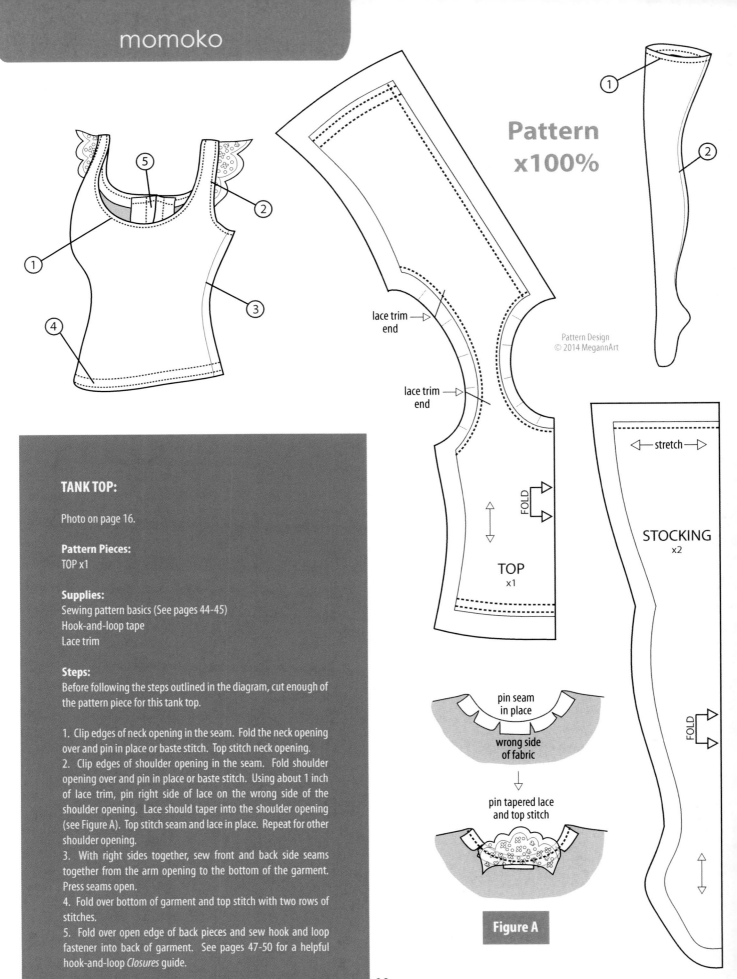

Pattern x100%

Pattern Design
© 2014 MegannArt

lace trim end →

lace trim end →

FOLD

TOP
x1

← stretch →

STOCKING
x2

FOLD

pin seam in place

wrong side of fabric

↓

pin tapered lace and top stitch

Figure A

TANK TOP:

Photo on page 16.

Pattern Pieces:
TOP x1

Supplies:
Sewing pattern basics (See pages 44-45)
Hook-and-loop tape
Lace trim

Steps:
Before following the steps outlined in the diagram, cut enough of the pattern piece for this tank top.

1. Clip edges of neck opening in the seam. Fold the neck opening over and pin in place or baste stitch. Top stitch neck opening.

2. Clip edges of shoulder opening in the seam. Fold shoulder opening over and pin in place or baste stitch. Using about 1 inch of lace trim, pin right side of lace on the wrong side of the shoulder opening. Lace should taper into the shoulder opening (see Figure A). Top stitch seam and lace in place. Repeat for other shoulder opening.

3. With right sides together, sew front and back side seams together from the arm opening to the bottom of the garment. Press seams open.

4. Fold over bottom of garment and top stitch with two rows of stitches.

5. Fold over open edge of back pieces and sew hook and loop fastener into back of garment. See pages 47-50 for a helpful hook-and-loop *Closures* guide.

STOCKINGS:

Photo on page 16.

Pattern Pieces:
STOCKING x2

Supplies:
Sewing pattern basics (See pages 44-45)

Steps:
Before following the steps outlined in the diagram, cut enough of the pattern piece for these stockings. Thin stretchable fabrics are recommended for this pattern.

1. Fold top side of the STOCKING over and top stitch. Repeat for other STOCKING pattern.
2. With right sides together, sew seam from top of STOCKING, down to the toes. Turn inside out and repeat for other cut STOCKING pattern.

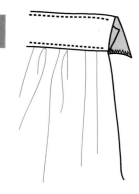

momoko

Pattern x100%

Figure B

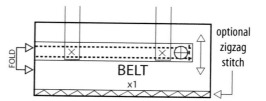

optional zigzag stitch

BELT
x1

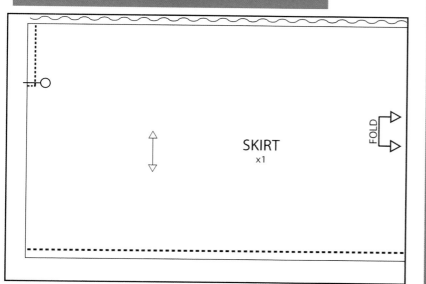

SKIRT
x1

FOLD

Pattern Design
© 2014 MegannArt

SKIRT WITH SUSPENDERS:

Photo on page 16.

Pattern Pieces:
SKIRT x1 and BELT x1

Supplies:
Sewing pattern basics (See pages 44-45)
Bead-and-loop closure
Approximately 8-1/2 inches of 3 mm wide ribbon
Two small buttons or seed beads

Steps:
Before following the steps outlined in the diagram, cut enough of each pattern piece for this skirt with suspenders.

1. Fold bottom side of SKIRT over and top stitch.
2. Where indicated on BELT piece, sew a zigzag stitch along the edge. This step is optional. It will avoid fraying of the belt on the inside of the garment later.
3. On the SKIRT, gather where indicated until gather is the length of the BELT. With right sides together, pin gathered fabric every 1/2 inch to inch to the BELT. Sew seam.
4. Fold BELT over seam and top stitch around front side of belt (see Figure B).
5. Cut two pieces of 3 mm wide ribbon into 4-1/4 inch long pieces. With about 1/4 inch of ribbon overlapping the front of the skirt, sew ribbon and button in place where indicated on the pattern with an "X". Repeat for other ribbon on the front side of the dress. By this stage, both ribbons should only be attached in the front. Test the length of the ribbon on doll and pin each ribbon in place on the inside of the back of skirt where indicated on pattern with an "X". Sew the straps in place with a needle and thread.
6. With right sides together, sew seam from bottom of skirt to —O point on pattern. Turn inside out. See pages 47-50 for a bead-and-loop *Closures* guide.

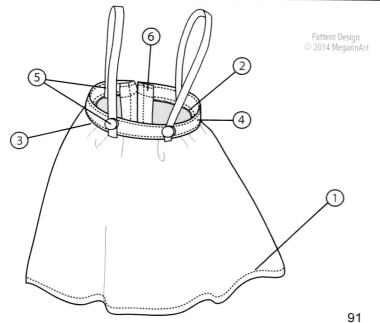

Photo Credits:

COVER: Tan skin Peak's Woods Fairy of Fairytales (FOF) Cheshire Goon. Face up by Peak's Woods. Wig by F-Styler. Resin eyes by Enchanted Doll. Bow tie by MegannArt.

PAGE 2: Natural skin Fairyland PukiPuki Cupid 1 Basic. Face up by Fairyland. Eyes original with doll. Boots by Ruby Red Galleria. Ball-jointed doll wig of unknown origin (no markings on inside of wig to indicate company), given to the author by a colleague.

PAGE 3: Fairyland PukiPuki Sugar. Face up by Fairyland. Eyes original with doll. Mohair wig by Kemper.

PAGES 4-5: Integrity Toys Dangerous To Know Kyori Sato. Ring by Integrity Toys. Bracelets and apple by MegannArt.

PAGES 6-7: Normal skin Peak's Woods Fairy of Fairytales (FOF) Hucky. Face up by Peak's Woods. Leeke World wig. Acrylic eyes. Shoes are from an unknown company and were found on eBay during a search for "YoSD shoes." Flower pin for hair by MegannArt.

PAGE 8: Integrity Toys Midnight Star Elise Jolie. Barbie Basics Collection 1 Accessory Pack 3 white boots by Mattel. Tiny hand-painted pots are from an unknown company, purchased at a second-hand store.

PAGE 9: Integrity Toys Irresistible Dania Zarr. Bird cage is from an unknown company, purchased from a second-hand store.

PAGE 10: momokoDOLL Happy Summer Guaranteed.

PAGES 10-11: PW-momoko ae <F.L.C.> 2013. Boots and hat by SEKIGUCHI. Bicycle is from an unknown company, purchased from Cost Plus World Market.

PAGE 12: Doll originally a Monster High Clawdeen Wolf by Mattel. Face up by Samantha Siakovich (anthrogirl on Den of Angels). Mohair wig by Kemper. Hair bow by MegannArt. Stardoll shoes by Mattel. Necklace by Tracy's Trinkets. Dog and chair from an unknown company and were given to the author.

PAGE 13: Fairyland PukiPuki Sugar. Face up by Fairyland. Eyes original with doll. Wig by Ruby Red Galleria.

PAGE 14: Integrity Toys Irresistible Dania Zarr. Business accessory by Mattel. Necklace by Tracy's Trinkets.

PAGE 15: Integrity Toys Dangerous To Know Kyori Sato. Telephone prop is a sharpener labeled "MADE IN HONG KONG" on the bottom with no other company information, purchased at a second-hand store.

PAGE 16: momokoDOLL Honey Wild. Shoes by PetWORKs. Necklace by Tracy's Trinkets. Frames are metal stickers by Momenta. Flower illustration is from the book, "A Year with the Wild Flowers" by author Edith Waddy, published by Wesleyan Conference Office of London. No illustrator credited. Published approximately in the 1870s. Recolored by MegannArt. Tiny cat illustration is from the book, "Baby's Annual Pictures and Stories for Little People," Published by D. Lothrop Company (1890). No artist or author identified. Oval border on tiny cat illustration by MegannArt.

PAGE 17: Doll originally a Monster High Draculaura by Mattel. Face up and hair restyling by Megann Zabel of MegannArt. Stardoll shoes by Mattel. Hand-painted wooden elephants from an unknown company and were given to the author.

PAGES 18-19: White skin Peak's Woods Fairy of Fairytales (FOF) Dorothy Young. Face up by Peak's Woods. Wig by Kemper. Resin eyes by Enchanted Doll. Small seed paper heart by Botanical Paperworks. Tree with gold leaves and stuffed bear are from unknown companies, purchased from a second-hand store.

PAGES 20-21: Doll originally a Monster High Frankie Stein by Mattel. Face up by Samantha Siakovich (anthrogirl on Den of Angels). Stardoll shoes by Mattel. Bracelets by MegannArt. Wooden cuckoo clock ornament is from an unknown company, purchased from a second-hand store.

PAGES 22-23: Tan skin Peak's Woods Fairy of Fairytales (FOF) Cheshire Goon. Face up by Peak's Woods. Wig by F-Styler. Resin eyes by Enchanted Doll. Shoes by DollHeart. Bow tie by MegannArt.

PAGE 25: White skin Peak's Woods Monthly Fairy Coco Rain. Face up by Peak's Woods. Eyes original with doll. Ball-jointed doll wig of unknown origin (no markings on inside of wig to indicate company), given to the author by a colleague. Gazebo prop is labeled "CE954 MADE IN CHINA" on the bottom with no other company information, purchased from a second-hand store.

PAGES 26: La Dee Da Tylie by Spin Master. Long gold earrings with diamonds by Tracy's Trinkets.

PAGE 27: Azone Picco Neemo Koron. Shoes by Azone. Small wooden picket fence by Darice.

PAGE 28: Pepper Parson Pinkie Cooper and the Jet Set Pets doll by The Bridge Direct. Shoes and bracelet original with doll. Necklace and hair bow by MegannArt.

PAGE 29: Normal skin To You Sara by Limhwa Dolls (EOS Doll, Ji-Youn). Acrylic eyes. Wig by Ruby Red Galleria.

PAGES 30: La Dee Da Tylie by Spin Master.

PAGE 31: Debut Silkstone Barbie by Mattel. Gold earrings by MegannArt.

PAGE 32: Deja Vu Emma Jean McGowen Basic (Black) doll used by permission of Tonner Doll Company, Inc. Necklace by MegannArt.

PAGE 33: Azone Picco Neemo Romantic Girly Chiika. Head ornament by MegannArt. Shoes are from an unknown company and were found on eBay during a search for "Kelly shoes."

PAGES 34-35: Kelly and Friends dolls Lil' Flyer Marisa, Singing Star Jenny, and Lil' Gentleman Tommy by Mattel. Kelly shoes by Mattel.

PAGE 36: Normal skin To You Sara by Limhwa Dolls (EOS Doll, Ji-Youn). Acrylic eyes. Wig by Ruby Red Galleria.

PAGE 37: Fun with Cherry Blossom Honee-B by Ruby Red Galleria. Wig original with doll. Small bear is from an unknown company and was found on eBay during a search for "miniature doll house."

PAGE 38: REVLON Ultra Basic Brunette doll used by permission of Tonner Doll Company, Inc. Skirt and earrings by MegannArt.

PAGE 39: Izzy as Wendy doll (Friends of Amelia Thimble) of Wilde Imagination, Inc. used by permission of Tonner Doll Company, Inc. Shoes original with doll.

PAGE 40: Mod Era Walk Lively Miss America Barbie by Mattel.

The author is not affiliated with these doll companies or any other manufacturers.

Suggested Resources:

Dolly Bureau: Doll Patterns and Fashion (Volume 1) by Megann R. Zabel

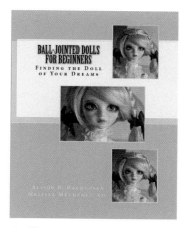

Ball-Jointed Dolls for Beginners by Alison Boyd Rasmussen, edited by Melissa Metheney

A Little More Ball-Jointed Dolls for Beginners by Alison Boyd Rasmussen

Alice: Out of the Box: A collection of Wonderland-themed dolls by Alison Boyd Rasmussen

Steffie: Out of the Box (Volume 1) by Alison Boyd Rasmussen

For more photos and resources, visit **dollybureau.com.**

Did you make a pattern from this book and want to share it? Go to dollybureau.com to find ways to post your work. Interested in contributing to future editions of Dolly Bureau? Want an opportunity to promote your work? Send and email to info@dollybureau.com.

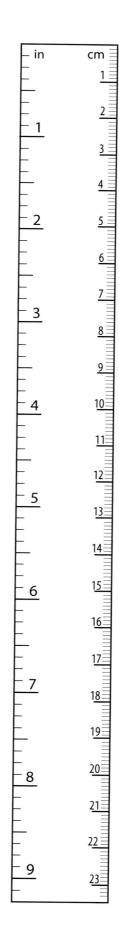

Made in the USA
Middletown, DE
13 December 2019